RED TEAM

DEVELOPMENT AND OPERATIONS

A practical guide

ZERO-DAY EDITION

Joe Vest and James Tubberville

©2019 Joe Vest and James Tubberville

Copyright notice: All rights reserved. No part of this book may be reproduced or transmitted in any form or by any means, electronic or mechanical, including photocopying, recording, or by any information storage and retrieval system without the written permission of the author, except where permitted by law.

http://redteam.guide

Authors' Statement

"A great deal of time and money is spent on protecting critical digital assets. Many organizations focus their security testing on compliance or limited scope reviews of a system. These limited tests often leave an organization with a false sense of security. Organizations that open themselves to an assessment of not only their technology but of their people and processes can significantly improve their security posture and adjust its limited security budget and resources to protect the most critical assets. Scenario-based testing and Red Team techniques can be used to determine how an organization really stands up to a realistic and determined threat." - Joe Vest and James Tubberville

Preface

This book is the culmination of years of experience in the information technology and cybersecurity field. Components of this book have existed as rough notes, ideas, informal and formal processes developed and adopted by the authors as they led and executed red team engagements over many years. The concepts described in this book have been used to successfully plan, deliver, and perform professional red team engagements of all sizes and complexities. Some of these concepts were loosely documented and integrated into red team management processes, and much was kept as tribal knowledge. One of the first formal attempts to capture this information was the SANS SEC564 Red Team Operation and Threat Emulation course. This first effort was an attempt to document these ideas in a format usable by others. The authors have moved beyond SANS training and use this book to detail red team operations in a practical guide.

The authors' goal is to provide practical guidance to aid in the management and execution of professional red teams. The term 'Red Team' is often confused in the cybersecurity space. The terms roots are based on military concepts that have slowly made their way into the commercial space. Numerous interpretations directly affect the scope and quality of today's security engagements. This confusion has created unnecessary difficulty as organizations attempt to measure threats from the results of quality security assessments. You quickly understand the complexity of red teaming by performing a quick google search for the definition, or better yet, search through the numerous definitions and interpretations posted by security professionals on Twitter. This book was written to provide a practical solution to address this confusion.

The Red Team concept requires a unique approach different from other security tests. It relies heavily on well-defined TTPs critical to the successful simulation of realistic threat and adversary techniques. Proper

Red Team results are much more than just a list of flaws identified during other security tests. They provide a deeper understanding of how an organization would perform against an actual threat and determine where a security operation's strengths and weaknesses exist.

Whether you support a defensive or offensive role in security, understanding how Red Teams can be used to improve defenses is extremely valuable. Organizations spend a great deal of time and money on the security of their systems. It is critical to have professionals who understand the threat and can effectively and efficiently operate their tools and techniques safely and professionally. This book will provide you with the real-world guidance needed to manage and operate a professional Red Team, conduct quality engagements, understand the role a Red Team plays in security operations. You will explore Red Team concepts in-depth, gain an understanding of the fundamentals of threat emulation, and understand tools needed you reinforce your organization's security posture.

Who is the best audience for this book?
- Security professionals interested in expanding their knowledge of Red Teaming
- Penetration testers or ethical hackers looking to understand how Red Teaming is different from other security testing types
- Defenders who want to understand offensive methodologies, tools, and techniques better
- Auditors who need to build relevant technical skills and understand how to measure success
- Red Team members looking to understand their craft as professionals better
- Threat hunters looking to understand better how red teaming can increase their ability to defend
- Computer Network Defense or Exploitation (CND/CNE) Teams
- Forensics specialists who want to understand offensive tactics better

- Information security managers who need to incorporate red team activities into their operations

In summary, this book will prepare you to:

- Learn what Red Teaming is and how it differs from other security testing engagements
- Understand the unique view of the offensive security field of Red Teaming and the concepts, principles, and guidelines critical to its success
- Design and create threat-specific goals to measure and train organizational defenders
- Learn to use the "Get In, Stay In, and Act" methodology to achieve operational impacts
- Design, operate, and run a professional red teaming program
- Make the best use of a Red Team and apply it to measure and understand an organization's security defenses

Acknowledgments

Writing this book has been an intense journey and many roadblocks have shown their face. Life doesn't stop and give you time to meet deadlines. Without the support of family, friends, coworkers, and the infosec community, this book would not have been written. Thank you all!

This book is a collection of thoughts, ideas, and experiences. Many of these ideas and concepts would not have been developed without the people worked with over the last ten years. We want to thank everyone who listened to us ramble on for what may have felt like hours. You are as much as part of this book as we are.

We especially need to thank family and close friends. Reading early drafts, listening to ramblings about security, giving advice, keeping us honest, and encouraging us to stay on track are just a few ways you helped. This book would not have been written without your encouragement and support. We thank and love you all!

We want to name everyone by name, but do not wish to miss someone unintentionally. We'll shake your hand or give you a hug the next time we see you.

We encourage all of you to reach for your goals.

How to use the book

This book was written to provide a practical approach to building and running a professional Red Team. The book is divided into chapters that roughly match the phases of a Red Team engagement. Chapters begin by diving into a specific topic to provide background and detail on various Red Team topics. Each chapter ends with key chapter takeaways and homework. The key chapter takeaways provide a brief chapter summary and homework lists the steps the reader should take to apply the specific topics. Working through the homework builds the elements needed for a professional Red Team. These elements can be used as a roadmap to help a team develop and grow.

Companion website (http://redteam.guide)

This book has a companion website, **http://redteam.guide.** This website hosts additional information, templates, guides, labs, and other useful information that helps enhance the book's contents.

Table of Contents

AUTHORS' STATEMENT V
PREFACE VII
ACKNOWLEDGMENTS X
HOW TO USE THE BOOK XI
    COMPANION WEBSITE (HTTP://REDTEAM.GUIDE) XI
TABLE OF CONTENTS 12
INTRODUCTION 15
    RED TEAMS IN SECURITY TESTING 31
    RED TEAMING ORGANIZATIONS 37
    KEY CHAPTER TAKEAWAYS 40
    HOMEWORK 40
ENGAGEMENT PLANNING 41
    COST AND FUNDING 41
    SCOPE 41
    DURATION 42
    PERSONNEL LABOR COST 43
    EQUIPMENT AND SOFTWARE COST 44
    TRAVEL COST 44
    PRE- AND POST-ENGAGEMENT COST 44
    FREQUENCY 45
    ENGAGEMENT NOTIFICATIONS 47
    ROLES AND RESPONSIBILITIES 49
    RULES OF ENGAGEMENT (ROE) 55
    MANAGING RISK 58
    THREAT PLANNING 60
    THREAT PROFILE 63
    CREATING A THREAT PROFILE BY DECOMPOSING A THREAT 68
    A REVIEW OF A BLACKHAT'S TRADECRAFT 72
    THREAT PERSPECTIVE 78
    THREAT SCENARIO 80
    THREAT EMULATION 82
    SCENARIO MODELS 83
    INDICATORS OF COMPROMISE 85

    Engagement Concepts 88
    Deconfliction 94
    Data Handling 98
    Key Chapter Takeaways 103
    Homework 103

ENGAGEMENT EXECUTION 104

    Data Repository 104
    Data Collection 108
    Tradecraft 114
    General Guidance 114
    Execution Concepts 122
    Tools and Tool Examples 128
    Command and Control (C2) 136
    Key Chapter Takeaways 150
    Homework 150

ENGAGEMENT CULMINATION 151

    Sanitization and Cleanup 151
    Operator Log Verification 153
    Pre-Report Briefings 154
    Key Chapter Takeaways 161
    Homework 161

ENGAGEMENT REPORTING 162

    Attack Flow Diagrams 163
    Observations vs. Findings 165
    Risk Rating and Metrics 166
    Risk Matrices Comparison 167
    Attack Narrative 178
    Key Chapter Takeaways 184
    Homework 184

SUMMARY 185

CONCLUSION 187

APPENDIX A: EXAMPLE TEMPLATES 188

APPENDIX B: THOUGHT EXERCISES 189

    Adversarial Mindset Challenge 189
    Mindset Challenge Comments and Answers 195

APPENDIX C: DECOMPOSING A THREAT EXERCISE 199

- Description 199
- Exercise Scenario 199
- Goal 199
- Resources 200
- Begin the Exercise 200
- Create a threat profile 205
- Possible Solution 206

GLOSSARY OF TERMS 208

Introduction

Designing, deploying, and managing a comprehensive security program is complex and challenging and, therefore, not an easy task for most. Organizations are influenced and pressured from multiple, often competing, sources. This pressure can come from customers, compliance, management, peers, finance, public opinion, and publicly available news, just to name a few. Even when faced with these challenges, organizations are generally able to overcome these pressures and implement what is *considered* to be a robust security program. Organizations can satisfy the various parties and, at least on paper, describe a security program designed to stop malicious cyber-attacks. As a result, audit and compliance checks pass, robust patch management systems are deployed, and vulnerability assessments and penetration tests are conducted. These are significant initial steps toward providing the means to defend a network from attack. Unfortunately, this often falls short in achieving the primary goal of preventing, detecting, and responding to real threats. Why? What is missing? The real question to consider is:

> Are organizations truly building security programs designed to address the threat?

A security program includes many components such as staff, policies, procedures, tools, management, oversight, incident response, etc. The program is designed and built with the assistance of members from several different divisions or job functions, all contributing their thoughts and security requirements. Security programs often use this strategy for ensuring a complete and holistic security program; however, what or who is often missing? Has anyone on the security operations team ever seen a bad guy? Has anyone on the team attacked or compromised a network? To what extent? To quote Peter in the movie Office Space[1]. *"I can't believe what a bunch of nerds we are. We're looking up money laundering in a dictionary."* Are teams designing defenses for an enemy they do not know or understand?

Is the threat included in security planning?

Good intentions by a group of intelligent people do not add up to understanding threats or how they operate. If the goal of security operations is to prevent, detect, respond, and recover against malicious actions, it only makes sense to include the opinions of those whom you are defending against. Unfortunately, security design often excludes the threat or threat perspective. This omission often leads to the mitigation or acceptance of risks not fully understood or revealed during traditional security testing and auditing. The result is a severe false sense of security. A real threat knows this and uses it to their advantage.

Consider This

Does a threat know a target has a robust security program?
Do threats perform actions that will trigger an alert or get them caught?
Are threats still successful?
If so, why are threats able to successfully achieve its goals and negatively impact an organization when that organization has a comprehensive security program? To understand this,
We must understand the threat to develop defenses properly.

---

[1] "Office Space (1999) - IMDb." https://www.imdb.com/title/tt0151804/.

The security industry uses the term threat, but what is a threat?

Dictionary.com[2] defines threat as:
a declaration of an intention or determination to inflict punishment, injury, etc., in retaliation for, or conditionally upon, some action or course; menace an indication or warning of probable trouble a person or thing that threatens.

ISO 27001[3] defines threat as:
A potential cause of an incident, that may result in harm of systems and organization.

NIST[4] defines threat as:
Any circumstance or event with the potential to adversely impact organizational operations (including mission, functions, image, or reputation), organizational assets, individuals, other organizations, or the Nation through an information system via unauthorized access, destruction, disclosure, modification of information, or denial of service. |

Let's walk through this in the context of cybersecurity threats. A threat is an event that has the potential to impact an organization adversely. Are security operations teams defending against this threat? A negative event? Perhaps, but consider including the term threat-actor when using threat. A threat-actor is the person or group of people behind an attack. A solid defensive strategy must defend against an intelligent threat-actor determined to cause damage to an organization and not just a potential event. People are behind cyber-attacks. When the defense considers the tactics, techniques, and procedures (TTPs) of intelligent threat-actors, they begin to understand the real threat. Defenders can then implement robust

---

[2] "Threat | Definition of Threat at Dictionary.com." https://www.dictionary.com/browse/threat.
[3] "ISO IEC 27000 2014 Information Security Definitions - Praxiom." https://www.praxiom.com/iso-27000-definitions.htm.
[4] "threat - Glossary | CSRC - NIST Computer Security Resource ...." https://csrc.nist.gov/glossary/term/threat.

security defenses that directly impact the ability a threat-actor has to perform harmful actions. Shifting security operations from the mindset of "Vulnerable" or "Not Vulnerable" and adopting an approach that focuses on threat actions will significantly improve the ability an organization has to not only prevent but also detect and respond to real threats. Diving into TTPs is the beginning of understanding security through the eyes of the threat. Organizations that use threat actions to drive their defensive TTPs can make life very difficult for threat-actors and even protect themselves against unknown or zero-day attacks.

Why do Threats Succeed?

Many organizations currently use audit and compliance, vulnerability assessments, and penetration testing to evaluate and measure risk to cyber-attack. Why bother with a new, threat-focused approach?

Isn't the identification and mitigation of vulnerabilities enough?

To answer, you must understand how a threat-actor thinks and acts. Remember, a threat is really an intelligent person determined to cause harm. It is NOT an exploit of a vulnerability, NOT a piece of malware, or NOT a phishing attack. These are merely the means a threat-actor may choose to achieve their end goal. The threat-actor assumes the target has a comprehensive security program and a suite of security tools (firewalls, intrusion detection systems, anti-virus, EDR, etc.) deployed with the intent of stopping cyber-attacks. A good threat-actor will likely assume an organization has deployed patches, conducted vulnerability assessments to reduce the exploit attack surface, and conducted penetration tests to identify attack paths. This understanding can significantly change the actions taken by a threat-actor. These actions can be quite different compared to the actions taken by a traditional security tester. Does the threat-actor fire up a port scanner and enumerate an entire network? Does a threat-actor run a vulnerability scanning tool to find an exploit? Attacks by threat-actors do not always follow the models adopted by traditional security testing. An attack is not scan -> exploit -> profit. An intelligent threat-actor evaluates what a target presents and uses weakness not always discovered through traditional security tests. A "good" threat-actor will take several controlled steps to gain access to a target, establish command and control, establish persistence, perform situational awareness, to ultimately achieve their desired goal. The people charged with defending an organization often ignore or misunderstand the steps taken by a threat-actor. This misunderstanding often leads to a focus on prevention, not detection. Defenders who do focus on detection may drown themselves in un-actionable default or vendor-generated logs and alerts. Have you ever heard a security operations analyst state, *"We have too many logs and alerts to respond!"* or *"We are just trying to keep up with ticket volume!"*? Why do organizations log what they log? Compliance? In case they are needed? Vendor's advice? Organizations are still missing a key piece to all threats; understanding their actions and TTPs.

Consider this scenario

After evaluating a target network, a threat-actor decides phishing is their chosen method to gain access. They send a phishing email to a small number of targeted individuals. The phish contains an excel attachment with a DDE based attack[5]. One of the email recipients opens the attachment. This launches malicious code and establishes command and control (C2). The threat-actor then performs a series of steps that includes situational awareness of current access, enumeration of potential new targets, and identification of lateral movement options to those targets. In

---

[5] "Reviving DDE: Using OneNote and Excel for Code Execution ...." 29 Jan. 2018, https://enigma0x3.net/2018/01/29/reviving-dde-using-onenote-and-excel-for-code-execution/.

this case, the threat finds clear text database credentials on an old test web application backup in a public share. The web application has no direct significance or critical data other than access to a test database with no critical data. It's just a test application. The credentials provide the means to laterally move to a test database server. Remember, the database doesn't have sensitive data but is part of the "server zone" in the network. Code execution on the database server provides elevated access. The situational awareness cycle repeats. The threat-actor discovers elevated credentials stored in memory on the database server. The threat extracts this credential material and uses to communicate with a Windows domain controller to extract an even greater elevated credential from a Windows domain controller using the dcsync[6] technique. The threat-actor repeats the situational awareness and enumeration cycle using the newly gained credentials from the domain controller. The intended target is identified and located on a sensitive file repository. The threat-actor prepositions themselves using the access and information gained and achieves its final objective by exfiltrating sensitive data from the network.

Answer the following questions as if you were part of the targeted organization.

- Is this scenario reasonable?
- Were opportunities presented to detect or prevent the threat?
- Could your current security program prevent, detect, or respond to this threat?
- Are you sure?
- Have you verified?
- If so, how?
- What techniques or indicators were left behind by this threat?

---

[6] "Hashdump without the DC using DCSync (because we all ...." 2 Oct. 2015, https://silentbreaksecurity.com/invoke-dcsync-because-we-all-wanted-it/.

Organizations often blame the end-user who clicked the link. This scenario indicates an organization's entire security model may depend on users not clicking a link in an email. What about the actions the threat took after the initial click? Many organizations do not intend to hinge all security on a single user, but the steps taken to defend systems often say otherwise.

> **Consider This**
>
> **A phishing attack leading to compromise is NOT the fault of an end-user but rather, insufficient security controls of a target environment.** End-users are often blamed for compromise due to a phishing attack. Security defenses are not intended to hinge on a user's click decision to click or not. If a user who falls victim to a phishing attack leads to system-wide compromise, that user already had the potential to elevate privileges or otherwise compromise the environment.

Why is this scenario successful?

Organizations often have the wrong mindset to security defense.

Users are blamed for clicking links
User education is only one piece of defense in security operations. Users will click. It's their job!

Policies, procedures, and compliance measure security
These are extremely important to a security program but often only represent the minimum needed to comply with a standard. Treat compliance as the stick at an amusement park. You must be "this tall" to ride.

Log everything; You never know what you need
Security operations often log a tremendous amount of unactionable data. Logging may be due to compliance requirements, vendor

recommendations, lack of understanding of data sources, or a 'better safe than sorry' mindset. This misunderstanding leads to bottlenecks and overburdened security analysts.

Patch, patch, patch. Threats only use exploits
A common misunderstanding or viewpoint is threats only use exploits. This is far from the truth. Patch management is an essential factor in a comprehensive security program that helps with attack surface reduction. Threats understand this and may change their tactics. This concept is further explored and discussed in the text as "exploitation without exploits".

Our security tools will save us
The security industry is very dependent on security tools. Unfortunately, many do not know how these tools work. The lack of understanding leads to poor tuning and misconfiguration. Tools should improve the efficiency and capability of our security defenders and analysts and not drive security operations directly. These are tools. A hammer and nails won't build a house without a carpenter.

There are numerous reasons why the above scenario is successful. These bullets are light-hearted attempts at humor; they are more often than not issues in practices and thought processes of real-world organizations.

How do we solve this dilemma?

We can solve through Red Teaming based exercises. Red Teaming captures the threat perspective. Inspired by military philosophy, many industries have discovered the virtue of "Red Teaming" a defensive capability, and that its effectiveness grows when tested under actual battlefield conditions. Merely studying a threat's tactics is less useful than actually experiencing them. Simulated threats build real confidence and muscle memory in network defenders and arm them with better situational awareness of tooling and tactics as well as lessons learned from simulated failure.

Red Teaming may be referred to as threat emulation, threat simulation, adversary emulation, adversary simulation, or some other phrase that expresses a threat-based approach to security testing.

Before we jump too deep into the concepts of red teaming, we must level set our definitions. A common lexicon is critical to keep everyone on the same page to ensure we maintain a common unbiased base of understanding. The authors of this book have seen misunderstood terms cause severe complications and missed expectations. Concepts will be defined and explained throughout this book. We begin by defining red teaming.

> Red Teaming is the process of using Tactics, Techniques, and Procedures (TTPs) to emulate a real-world threat with the goals of training and measuring the effectiveness of the people, processes, and technology used to defend an environment.

Assumptions, bias, misunderstandings, and disbelief have a significant impact on the security operations of an environment. Red Teams provide formidable, honest assessments of internal practices and security controls by challenging assumptions, disregarding norms, and exposing atrophy and bias. An unbiased analysis using Red Teaming measures the gap between "what is" and "what should be". The application of red teaming provides unbiased ground truth and a deep understanding of security operations as a whole.

Red Teaming epitomizes the practice of attacking problems from an adversarial point of view. This mindset challenges an idea to help prove its worth, identify weaknesses, or identify areas to improve. Complex systems are developed, designed, and implemented by skilled, trusted professionals. These individuals are well respected and trusted in their field and are highly capable of designing and developing functional systems. Although these systems are highly functional and capable, the ideas, concepts, and thoughts can sometimes be "boxed in," leading to incorrect assumptions about how a system honestly operates. People build systems, and people make assumptions about capability, functionality, and security. These assumptions lead to flaws in which a threat may take advantage.

Red Teaming provides a means to challenge and test conventional wisdom and thought. A few standard methods to apply Red Teaming scenarios are:

Tabletop exercises – An activity where key individuals walk through a simulated situation to answer "what if" questions. Actual technical testing does not occur. Discussions of potential outcomes are explored and examined in an open discussion format.
Physical attacks – An attack on a physical resource, such as a facility or building, to test scenarios based on attack paths involving physical assets.
Human attacks – An attack that involves social engineering and the manipulation of people to achieve Red Team goals.
Cyber exercises – A Red vs. Blue exercise designed to train or evaluate staff and security operation defenses. Exercises can range from a focuses offensive threat scenario to a full Red vs. Blue war game.
Full-scale cyber operation – The most realistic attack an organization can endure outside of an attack from a real threat. The elements of the

operation collectively assess all aspects of a specific scenario. The scenario drives the need and may leverage physical, human, and cyber weaknesses to accomplish desired objectives.

Red Teaming does not focus on a vulnerability or weakness as a single "finding." During a Red Team engagement, an operator may find an unpatched or misconfigured system. This flaw may be used to the team's advantage to provide a more extensive compromise into a network or to pivot from the vulnerable system to achieve a specific goal or may not be used at all. Although a single unpatched or misconfigured system may give a Red Team Operator the means to compromise a network, it is just a means to an end. This is a crucial distinguisher for Red Teaming.

Red Team engagements focus on specific goals and objectives.

These goals may include compromising an application or network, stealing data, emulating a specific target, measuring the effectiveness of technical defenses, measuring the effectiveness of a security team, etc. The vulnerabilities and weaknesses identified during an assessment may need to be addressed and mitigated, but this is not the focus of Red Teaming. Red Teaming focuses on the bigger picture by providing insight into a target's detection and response capabilities. It gives understanding Mean-Time to Detect (MTTD) and Mean-Time to Recover (MTTR) from individual breaches. It exercises the relationship between its incident response and threat hunting teams by testing network defenders and their tools in ways that cannot be achieved through traditional threat intelligence, literature, or structured testing.

The following categories summarize Red Teaming goals.

Measuring the effectiveness of the people, processes, and technology used to defend a network

When a Red Team uses real-world attack techniques against a target's production network, the extent of the organization's defenses are challenged. For example, an engagement has the goal of stealing critical data from a target. A targeted phishing attack tests the end user's willingness to participate in an attack. The payload of the attack tests the network and host defenses against the delivery of malware and ultimately against code execution. If the attack does trigger a defensive control, the response measures the defender's actions in identifying, responding, or stopping the attack. Red teaming provides a means to measure security operations as a whole and not only focus on technical controls.

Training or measuring defensive or security operations

> "We don't rise to the level of our expectations; we fall to the level of our training." - Archilochus, Greek Poet, around 650 BC

Training the Blue Team (defenders of a network) is one of the most valuable aspects of Red Teams. Without training, how are defenders expected to defend against a real attack? Classroom exercises and conceptual training is valuable; however, Red Teams provide the ability for defensive operations to build skills against a threat in a safe, productive environment. Leadership that expects their defending team to respond to that threat without practice and successfully defend is fooling themselves. This form of training is more hands-on than typical security courses. The real-world practice of people using technology and following their processes is needed to understand security operation's ability to defend.

Testing and understanding specific threats or threat scenarios

A Red Team can execute and emulate a current, new, or custom threat as part of an engagement to test or validate the effectiveness of security controls. Threat emulation scenarios distinguish red teaming from other types of security assessments and can be used to understand an organization's posture against various threats. This approach provides the means to test scenarios based on new undiscovered threats or zero-day exploits. A great example is the EternalBlue[7] exploit. This exploit involved remote code execution using the SMB protocol, a key protocol used in Microsoft environments. Before the exploit was known, a Red Team could have easily designed a scenario where an attacker was able to propagate over the SMB protocol to measure the impact of this type of dangerous attack. Red teams don't need (or shouldn't) wait for a threat to develop and attack paths. Custom scenarios are a great way to understand current and future threats. More information can be found on ExternalBlue in CVE-2017-0144.

> **Remember This**
>
> Red Teams are used to measure the effectiveness of the people, processes, and technology used to defend a network, train or measure a Blue Team (defensive security operations), and test and understand specific threats or threat scenarios.

We've described what Red Teams do, but let's give them a definition to add to our common lexicon. A Red Team is an independent group that, from the perspective of a threat or adversary, explores alternative plans and operations to challenge an organization to improve its effectiveness.

Red Teams perform actions during a Red Teaming engagement outlined by the Rules of Engagement (ROE). We will discuss these rules in detail

---

[7] "CVE-2017-0144 - The MITRE Corporation." https://cve.mitre.org/cgi-bin/cvename.cgi?name=CVE-2017-0144

later. For now, think of them as a guide used by a Red Team as to how they should conduct actions. Red Teams are independent groups that are technically skilled and capable of executing a threat based-plan safely and professionally.

We keep describing Red Teams as "independent." Why? As discussed, many organizations or groups have significant biases and assumptions based solely on unproven or unconfirmed information. An independent Red Team, unobstructed by the biases of the target, can provide a clean review, fresh perspective, and accurate assessment of how a threat may cause an impact on various business functions. This team may be an external consultant or an internal team managed and operated separately from the rest of the organization. Independent reviews are invaluable in determining real-world risks and consequences and a key component of Red Teaming.

> **Consider This**
>
> **Independent Red Teams are invaluable in determining real-world risks and potential impacts.**
>
> Independence allows the Red Team to accurately review or assess while limiting many of the biases and assumptions of the target.

What is the difference between a Red Team and a real-world attacker? A Red Team will provide a report, or other deliverables, with the goal of understanding threat-based risks. Organizations that use Red Teams effectively do not need to wait and learn from a real-world breach. Red Teams are beneficial in analyzing systems for security weaknesses that may not be known or understood. The mindset and thought processes used by a professional Red Team Operator can break through common assumptions that severely weaken a system's security. Red Teams ask the "what if" questions to challenge system defenses at its core. Effectively using Red Teams can bring to light security flaws that have plagued a system for years and allow an organization to develop highly effective mitigating solutions.

Although there are tremendous benefits to Red Teams, they can be challenging to use. They are commonly used in name only. The activities performed during an engagement are no more than a vulnerability test or penetration test. The output may be something as simple as a list of findings. Red Teams must be able to think and act like a threat being portrayed. These engagements could be a gloves-off, advanced threat, or limited actions to emulate a single or straightforward threat. We will discuss how to do this by "adjusting the volume" of attacks and Indicator of Compromise (IOC) management later. For now, understand that a Red Team must operate within its rules and boundaries and focus on goals outlined in the engagement plan.

Red Teaming is about the overall story. Red Teams can document vulnerabilities and weaknesses identified during an assessment but focus on the whole story of the attacker throughout an engagement.

Consider This

Assumptions, bias, misunderstandings, and disbelief have a considerable impact on the security failures of an environment.

An unbiased Red Team helps measure the gap between "what is" and "what should be" to get to the truth of security operations as a whole.

Let's consider the following.

During early red team scenario planning, an organization's security leadership describes who has access to their accounting systems. They say, "5 people in accounting have access to the accounting system". In their minds, this is what "**Is**." When planning a threat scenario, you must think this is what "**Should Be**." This scenario is the perfect opportunity for a Red Team to validate assumptions in a professional and unbiased approach. The goal is not to prove that you can 'hack' into the system but to understand what "**Is**" vs. "**Should Be**."

5 people in accounting have access to the accounting system

20 accounts have admin access to the accounting system

Another way to describe this:

Is – The actual truth about the security stance of an organization. (E.g., 20 People have access to the sensitive accounting system.)

Should be – The perceived security stance of an organization. (E.g., only 5 people in accounting can access the sensitive accounting system.)

Challenging assumptions is a fundamental concept of red teaming.

Red Teams in Security Testing

Vulnerability assessment, penetration testing, and Red Teaming are commonly (yet erroneously) used interchangeably and fall under the general category of ethical hacking. This classification may be adequate for high-level conversations about security, but distinctions must be made. Security professionals and clients of security services will continue to blur the lines between these assessment types if differences are not made. We do ourselves a disservice by loosely defining terms. This hurts the security industry and the professionals themselves. This is more reason to level set definitions and come to a common understanding. Misunderstanding of assessment types has led to low-quality assessments claiming to be high-end. Terms must be defined early in an engagement to set expectations and deliver the service a client need.

Vulnerability Assessment

According to NIST Special Publication 800-53 (Rev. 4)[8], a vulnerability assessment is a "Systematic examination of an information system or product to determine the adequacy of security measures, identify security deficiencies, provide data from which to predict the effectiveness of

---

[8] "NIST SP 800-53 - NIST Page." 4 Apr. 2013,
https://nvlpubs.nist.gov/nistpubs/SpecialPublications/NIST.SP.800-53r4.pdf.

proposed security measures, and confirm the adequacy of such measures after implementation." In short, a vulnerability assessment is an analysis of a system that focuses on finding vulnerabilities and prioritizing them by risk.

The verification of identified vulnerabilities is left to the output of tools and the analyst's best judgment. The validation or exploitation of a vulnerability is not performed during a vulnerability assessment. When compared with Red Team engagements, vulnerability assessments are like good housekeeping. The mitigations applied due to the result of a vulnerability assessment are an effort in attack surface reduction with the intent to reduce the ability a threat has to gain an advantage of an identified flaw. A Red Teamer or threat assumes these types of assessments are being performed and mitigated appropriately. These steps in mitigation do impact the threat landscape and may reduce attack paths, but does not directly address the threat. It's best to consider vulnerability assessments as an effort in attack surface reduction.

Consider This

Red Teams rarely, if ever, run standard vulnerability assessment tools.

These tools are loud and generate more traffic than a Red Team engagement is willing to accept. If a vulnerability assessment tool MUST be used, there should be a question asked as to the type of security assessment being conducted, or they should be run with high focus from a "burned" attack location. Vulnerability assessments are still a critical component to security program but are quite different in scope and goals of a red team engagement.

Penetration Test

According to NIST Special Publication 800-53 (Rev. 4) CA-8 1, Penetration testing is defined as "… a specialized type of assessment conducted on information systems or individual system components to identify vulnerabilities that could be exploited by adversaries...". In other words, penetration testing is an authorized simulated attack against a system designed to identify and measure risks associated with the exploitation of a target's attack surface. This may sound like a red team engagement. The differences are often misunderstood but critical to the success of both.

Penetration testing takes a vulnerability assessment to the next level by introducing exploitation into the test. The goal of a penetration test is to determine the risk associated with vulnerabilities and flaws. A penetration test can look and feel very similar to a Red Team engagement, and in many cases, use the same tools. These similarities should not cause anyone to confuse the two. Penetration tests focus on exploiting weaknesses to determine business risk. It is common for a penetration test to explore a wide range of vulnerabilities to discover their risks. During a Red Team engagement, flaws will be exploited but only to the degree needed to achieve the goals or objectives. If a single vulnerability allows a Red Team to move forward, the team only uses this to move forward. The other twenty flaws found (by the Red Team or a previous vulnerability assessment) will be documented but may remain un-actioned during the Red Team engagement. Penetration testing, although more narrowly focused than a vulnerability assessment, has a much broader focus than a Red Team engagement. Like a vulnerability assessment, mitigation performed after a penetration test reduces the attack surface. This mitigation is an effective way to make it more difficult for attackers but does not minimize operational risk to zero. Attack surface reduction efforts are good at limiting a threat's ability to operate but do not measure a threat's ability to impact an organization. Penetration tests should be considered an effort in attack path validation with a goal to reduce the attack surface.

Penetration tests are often driven to support audit requirements, such as those for PCI/DSS[9] or HIPAA[10]. Red Teaming is typically not driven by compliance but by the desire to fully test an organization's ability to defend, respond, and react to a threat.

Risk to business operations is arguably the most critical consideration in measuring overall security risk. Security assessments that map findings and observations to operational risk can gain the support needed to make a significant improvement. Let's compare these types of assessments in terms of operational risk. An inverted triangle can illustrate the relationship of Red Teaming, Penetration Testing, and Vulnerability Assessments in terms of organizational or operational risk. The depth and breadth of each security assessment type, as can be seen, is quite different.

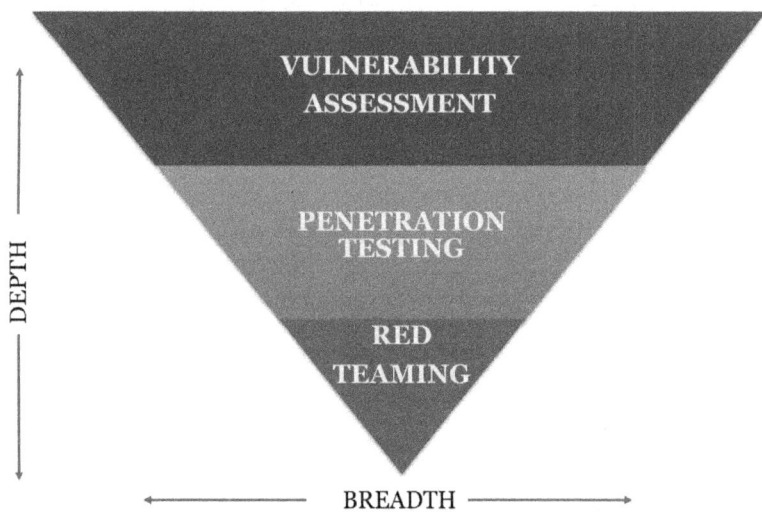

Vulnerability assessments tend to be broad in coverage but narrow in scope. Consider a vulnerability assessment of where the goal is to measure

---

[9] "PCI Security Standards Council." https://www.pcisecuritystandards.org/.
[10] "Health Information Privacy | HHS.gov." https://www.hhs.gov/hipaa/index.html.

all workstations in an enterprise. The scope is very broad but not very deep in the context of organizational risks. What can be said about the risk to operations when flaws are identified? Organizational risk can only be understood at the workstation level? The overall risk to an organization can be extrapolated to some degree but generally stays at that workstation level. Vulnerability assessments are good at reducing attack surface but do not provide much detail in terms of organizational risk. This common misunderstanding leads to vulnerability assessment being used to mismeasure security risk.

Penetrations tests take vulnerability assessments to the next level by exploiting and proving out attack paths. Although penetration tests may often look and feel like a red team engagement at the technical level, the critical difference lies in the goals and intent. The purpose of a penetration test is to execute an attack against a target system to identify and measure risks associated with the exploitation of a target's attack surface. Consider a penetration test against the external boundary of a network. A penetration tester exploits an identified flaw that allows inbound access to the target organization. From a penetration testing standpoint, this was the identification of a deficiency. What does this mean to the organization? What is the risk? If this flaw is mitigated, how does this impact organizational risk? The organizational risks can be indirectly measured as a flaw that allows a threat to gain remote access, but more severe risks to operations must be extrapolated from this attack. Mitigation will help address technical deficiencies and reduce the attack surface. What about the people and processes or detection and response actions? Will this type of attack be detected in the future, or is the organization playing a "whack-a-mole" game with individual vulnerabilities? Plugging holes is good and does reduce the attack surface, but this is where red teaming enters. Red Teaming focuses on security operations as a whole and includes people, processes, and technology. Red teaming focuses explicitly on goals related to training blue teams or measuring how security operations can impact a threat's ability to operate. Technical flaws are secondary to understanding how the threat was able to impact an organization's operations or how security operations were able to impact a threat's ability to operate.

Comparison Summary

Method	Description	Goal in Terms of Risk
Penetration Test	An attack against a system, network, or application designed to identify and measure risks associated with the exploitation of a target's attack surface. **Think: Attack path validation**	Attack surface reduction
Vulnerability Assessment	An assessment used to identify the adequacy of security measures, identify security deficiencies, and confirm the mitigations are in place with the goal of reducing a target's attack surface **Think: Flaw identification**	Attack surface reduction
Red Team Engagement	The process of using Tactics, Techniques, and Procedures (TTPs) to emulate a real-world threat with the goals of training or measuring the effectiveness of the people, processes, and technology used to defend an environment.	Training and measuring the effectiveness of the people, processes, and technology (security operations)

	Think: Measure security operation's capabilities as a whole	

Red Teaming Organizations

The NIST has provided general guidance in the form of the Cybersecurity Framework[11] for improving critical infrastructure cybersecurity. This framework provides a common taxonomy and mechanism for organizations to:

1. Describe their current cybersecurity posture
2. Describe their target state for cybersecurity
3. Identify and prioritize opportunities for improvement within the context of a continuous and repeatable process
4. Assess progress toward the target state
5. Communicate among internal and external stakeholders about cybersecurity risk

This framework presents industry standards, guidelines, and practices in a manner that allows for communication of cybersecurity activities and outcomes across the organization from the executive level to the implementation/operations level. The framework core consists of five concurrent and continuous functions: Identify, Protect, Detect, Respond, Recover. When considered together, these functions provide a high-level, strategic view of the lifecycle of an organization's management of cybersecurity risk. The framework core identifies underlying key categories and subcategories for each function. It matches them with example informative references, such as existing standards, guidelines, and practices for each subcategory. For more details, visit

---

[11] "Cybersecurity Framework | NIST." https://www.nist.gov/cyberframework.

https://www.nist.gov/cyberframework/cybersecurity-framework-faqs-framework-components.

In terms of Red Teaming, this document focuses on how Red Teaming can be used by an organization to understand its ability to Identify, Protect, Detect, Respond, and Recover against a threat. These categories are where we in the security industry should focus. Detection and response capabilities are vital and arguably the point of a security operations.

Identify – The Identify Function are foundational for effective use of the Framework. The organization has associated business context, functions, assets, people and technologies with potential weaknesses, vulnerabilities, and threats to ascertain risks.

Protect – The Protect function supports the ability to limit or contain the impact of a potential cybersecurity event. The organization is prepared and configured to prevent intrusion, exploitation, or manipulation of information.

Detect – The Detect function enables the timely discovery of cybersecurity events. The organization conducts reliable monitoring and identification of unauthorized activity or entities.

Respond – The Respond function supports the ability to contain the impact of a potential cybersecurity incident. The organization performs accurate identification and analysis of detected activities resulting in effective reporting and responses.

Recover – The Recover function supports timely recovery to normal operations to reduce the impact from a cybersecurity incident. Capabilities are effectively restored when operational processes/productions have been impaired.

PDRR Observation and Measurement Coverage

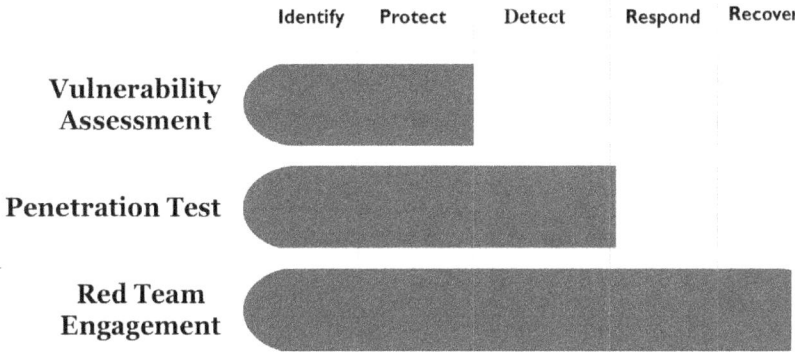

This diagram helps illustrate IPDRR coverage per engagement type.

Vulnerability assessments provide an organization the measure or understand the ability to identify or protect against a threat. This great but does not provide the means to understand security operations as a whole. Vulnerability assessments tend to focus on preventive controls.

Because penetration testing focuses on attack path validation, they can be used to measure not only identification or protection but detection of threat activity and possibly a bit of response. In general, penetration tests are scoped for maximum coverage is a relatively short time. These tests lead to further understanding of protection and detection against threat activity but do little to understand response or recovery.

Red Teaming allows an organization to explore all aspects of threat activity fully. Red Teaming provides the needed stimulation to engage security operations as a whole. Red Teaming can employ an organization to enable security operations (Blue Team) to utilize their TTPs through identification, protection, detection, response, and recovery from a threat. The level of measurement is shaped by the engagement plan and determined by the goals.

Key Chapter Takeaways

Red Teaming is the process of using Tactics, Techniques, and Procedures (TTPs) to emulate a real-world threat with the goals of training and measuring the effectiveness of the people, processes, and technology used to defend an environment.

Red teaming focuses on goals related to training blue teams or measuring how security operations can impact a threat's ability to operate. Technical flaws are secondary to understanding how the threat was able to impact an organization's operations or how security operations were able to impact a threat's ability to operate. Vulnerability assessments and penetration tests are focus on technical flaws that result in mitigation and attack surface reduction.

Consider This

Red Teaming may use offensive security techniques but is not offensive in nature. It is arguably part of the security defensive community.

Red cannot exist without Blue

Homework

1. Develop a lexicon of terms to maintain a common unbiased base of understanding that can be shared and referenced among internal and external stakeholders.
2. Create or adopt a definition of red teaming and store in the lexicon.
3. Adopt the "Is" vs "Should be" approach when developing threat-based scenarios
4. Perform the Adversarial Mindset Challenge in the Appendix to better understand the adversarial point of view.

Engagement Planning

All engagements must start with Engagement Planning, the first step in a Red Team engagement. It is not possible to conduct a professional and successful execution without fully understanding the goals and scope of the engagement, understanding the resources required to execute, and creating a solid plan.

Cost and Funding

As with any security effort, cost and funding are significant influencers in planning, scheduling, and executing a Red Team engagement. Several factors contribute to the overall cost and scope of an engagement. Each element should be carefully reviewed and documented explicitly in a contract or agreement. Regardless of team status (internal or external service provider), each factor applies.

Scope

Scope plays the most significant role in the overall cost of an engagement. Consider scoping a vulnerability assessment. There is often a considerable benefit and need to conduct a full-scope, in-depth review of every node in an environment. The equipment and software employed are usually part of the price (less additional licensing requirements), setup and configuration are already being conducted, and the addition of target space to the contract is generally cost-effective. This scoping effort is arguably straight forward and typically broken into the asset type being assessed.

Scoping could be split into workstations, servers, network components, or any logical asset category.

Now consider scoping a Red Team engagement. There are significant differences between an in-depth assessment of 1,000 nodes vs. one of 14,000 nodes. Accurate assumptions about the environment can be made based upon the data obtained from a few similar nodes; however, this data does not necessarily enable the Red Team to meet the objectives of the engagement. In general, as a target environment grows, so does the complexity of its security controls (and ideally its effectiveness). Sometimes, that complexity benefits the environment. Other times, it introduces weaknesses a Red Team may use advantageously to gain access or achieve threat-based goals. In either case, the Red Team has to manage the complexity of tactics to test and validate the overall threat strategy accurately. Red Teams are known for leveraging multiple systems or data points and "bending" configurations to meet the engagement's needs. Common security tools and applications don't regularly discover many of these flaws or paths. This understanding drives scope development toward a scenario rather than testing every node in a target environment using standard security testing tools. The scope should always directly and effectively support the operational objectives being measured.

Duration

The duration can be a set time frame as determined by the target or the Red Team; however, it is recommended that duration be set after the target objectives, requirements, and scope are determined. A realistic time frame can then be placed in the context of the scope, and be increased or decreased as required. It is essential not to use the timeframe to set scope. Arbitrarily setting a deadline can negatively impact the quality of an engagement scope by imposing artificial constraints. Although this is best practice, and duration should be set after the goals and scope are determined, it is helpful to have guidelines. You can use a period of two to four weeks for most engagements. This is a good starting point but must be adjusted based on the actual scope.

Focus Area

The two-to-four week recommendation is for estimating an individual engagement, which may be part of a larger campaign composed of multiple engagements. The goals must be considered when determining scope duration.

Personnel Labor Cost

Simultaneously while determining the scope and duration, Red Team leadership should estimate the number of personnel required for an engagement. These steps must be simultaneous as they depend on each other. When sizing a Red Team, you must consider the number, size, and length of engagements. The most basic Red Team engagement will consist of at least two individuals. A recommended standard starting size for planning is four individuals: three operators and one lead. Adjust the number up or down based on the size, length, and goals.

How can you adjust the scope using a factor of time or personnel? Consider this example; an engagement is scoped for six weeks using three operators against a target network that has 14,000 nodes. This engagement could be extended to eight weeks by reducing operators or may be reduced to four weeks by adding staff. This elasticity of time and personnel should be considered when planning to help address finance, schedule, and other limitations. There are limits and diminishing returns to this elasticity. Adjustments could compromise the ability to achieve engagement goals. It is recommended to always have a minimum of two dedicated operators for an engagement.

Equipment and Software Cost

Red Teams must maintain a common toolset ready to be leveraged on any engagement. The toolset can be comprised of both free and paid tools. This toolset can be further customized to meet the specific needs once an engagement has been scoped (or contracted if external). During many engagements, a target has an obscure piece of equipment, tool, or software within the target environment that requires a specialized hardware device or software interface. It is recommended that the target provides access to a reference system for Red Team use to reduce cost. If this option is not available, or the target decides that a goal is to understand how the Red Team obtains access, the additional overhead and cost may be rolled into the overall engagement costs. Customization of tools, specialized software, or hardware must be identified early during scope planning to capture impact to scope.

Travel Cost

Travel cannot be forgotten during planning. Funds must be allocated if an engagement is conducted at a specific target site or other remote location. These funds must include lodging, flights, local transportation, per diem costs, and miscellaneous expenses. For U.S. based teams, following GSA travel and per diem rates can be a good starting point to set travel budgets. Many organizations will use these rates and optionally add a percentage as a benefit and incentive to lessen the stress and burden of travel. For instance, it can be common to use GSA rates x 1.25. This has been a successful method to provide operators a good rate to cover lodging, meals, and incidentals.

Pre- and Post-Engagement Cost

Inexperienced teams often fail to allocate time and funds for pre- and post-engagement (non-execution time) activities. Most engagements require some form of information or intelligence gathering (OSINT), and passive target reconnaissance before execution. They also need time for infrastructure preparation and, occasionally, custom tool development. They all require planning before execution and analysis and reporting following execution. Don't forget to account for these efforts in the planning and costing/budgeting process.

This section does not cover every possible element required to appropriately budget, fund, or quote a Red Team engagement. It is written to prompt thought and discussion on the actual costs and expected line items of an engagement. Actual planning takes time and repetition to develop an effective process.

Frequency

A Red Team engagement can be a very stressful experience. People can react negatively or defensively when their character, tools, or processes are brought into question. Even a well-managed engagement where individual attribution is kept to a minimum can place tremendous stress on staff. Doing this too often may not provide the organization time to apply mitigations, may cause the organization to treat the results with little regard, or result in poor morale and few positive benefits. Testing too infrequently can be just as damaging as testing too frequently. When testing is conducted too infrequently, the organization can become complacent and lax in its security operations. Red Team engagements typically fall into three categories: Single, Periodic, or Continuous. The appropriate frequency depends on the target organization and the goals of the engagement.

Single

Performing a Red Team engagement as a single activity is typically done for organizations new to Red Teaming or those with large footprints and limited resources. It allows them to get their feet wet without a significant commitment. A one-time engagement can be as simple or complex as needed. Organizations that desire a one-time Red Team engagement may not know specifically what they need. An effective Red Team will interview and question an organization's management to best determine the need and requirement. If the Red Team does not guide this discussion, an engagement is likely to be at risk of becoming just another vulnerability assessment or penetration test. One-time engagements are a great way to introduce organizations to Red Teaming as long as the planning is managed and focused on Red Teaming goals and objectives.

Periodic

Periodic, annual, or bi-annual Red Team engagements are very common. Mature organizations that perform comprehensive Red Team engagements balance the stimulus needed to keep security operations sharp and the time needed to improve defenses. When performing an annual engagement, be cautious not to treat it as a compliance audit. It will be tempting to just go through the motions. When testing becomes routine, an organization may not treat the results as seriously as a one-off test. To combat this complacency, engagements should be challenging and engaging. They should focus on severe areas of risk and not be "just another test to see if the bad guys can get in." Focused scenarios, the strategic use of white carding (to be discussed later), and incorporating current threats will keep an engagement fresh and provide better results.

Continuous

Continuous Red Teaming is a newer concept. Think of this as persistent threat emulation. When an organization has a Red Team constantly attacking and engaging its network, it can understand weaknesses associated with long-term advanced and persistent threats. Constant does not mean 24 hours a day / 365 days a year. It means that a Red Team's goals are spread out over some time. Goals could be in weeks, months, or even years instead of over a one or two-week engagements. This approach allows a team to perform more realistic actions, attempt to remain in the network for a more extended period, and position themselves in ways a real threat would use to cause severe damage to an organization. They are also able to emulate actual threat activities and timelines. In this model, what happens if the team is not detected? The team can use operational impacts. These are the steps taken to impact an organization to elicit a response directly. A Red Team can expose their activity just enough to cause a reaction from security operations. Red Teams can turn up or down their activity as needed only to expose what they want. They can provide the defenders an opportunity to learn, provide metrics and measurements to management, and maintain access to conduct future operations. Continuous operations come at the cost of time, effort, and money and take more resources than any other testing type. Mature organizations or organizations with serious threats are the best candidates for continuous operations.

Engagement Notifications

When planning a Red Team engagement, a decision about whom to inform must be made. Will only a few trusted individuals know their network is under attack? Or, will the organization as a whole be aware? Neither option is better over the other. The decision of notification based on engagement goals or the engagement type. In the case of Red-on-Blue exercises, the decision is easy. Everyone knows. A choice must be made when performing a Red Team engagement against a live, active target. This decision can have a considerable impact on the results and must be made carefully.

Announced Red Team Engagement

The organization (or at least the security operations team) has the knowledge that an engagement is underway.

This can impact an engagement in the following ways.

- An organization may increase security, patch systems, change passwords, or otherwise prepare for a known attack. This can have a dramatic impact on the results.
- Planning can include all key members of an organization. This helps ensure the critical assets are included, and the Red Team goals can be set accordingly.
- Fears of a rogue Red Team can be dealt with early through effective communication. This typically leads to a more in-depth engagement where risks can be explored with well-planned rules of engagement.

Unannounced Red Team Engagement

The organization (especially the security operations team) does not know that an engagement is underway.

This can impact an engagement in the following ways.
- An organization will act and respond as it would on any given day. This provides very realistic results by measuring the actual posture of security operations.
- Fear of the unknown causes some organizations to react with the "sky is falling" mentality. This fear may cause unintended self-inflicted damages if policies and procedures are not followed.
- Goals and targets may not be included in the planning. When only a small number of an organization's team is part of planning, critical assets may be missed and not included in the scope. This oversight can cause an engagement to lose focus on areas that may expose an organization to considerable risk.

How To Decide?

The following two tips can be used to answer the question about choosing announced or unannounced.
1. If the overall goal is to measure the effectiveness of an organization's security operations, start the planning with an unannounced

engagement. Even with the limitations, the results will be the most accurate and realistic in terms of understanding a threat's impact
2. If the overall goal is to measure the effectiveness of a specific capability, tool, process, or technology, start the planning with an announced engagement. When goals are specific or targeted, including the defenders can ensure the scope and rules are adequately designed to achieve the desired results.

Red Team Tip

Announced vs. Unannounced Notification

1) If the overall goal is to measure the effectiveness of an organization's security operations, start the planning with an unannounced engagement. Even with the limitations, the results will be the most accurate and realistic in terms of understanding a threat's impact

2) If the overall goal is to measure the effectiveness of a specific capability, tool, process, or technology, start the planning with an announced engagement. When goals are specific or targeted, including the defenders can ensure the scope and rules are adequately designed to achieve the desired results.

Roles and Responsibilities

An effective Red Team is comprised of a team of individuals who can contribute to the overall success. Diversity is crucial, but the team as a whole must be comprised of the core operator traits. A team can be even more successful when multiple team members contribute in various areas. In addition to the Red Team itself, successful execution of an engagement requires the involvement of numerous roles and groups.

White Cell

(Typically used during "game style" execution)

The White Cell primarily enforces the Rules of engagement to ensure neither Red Team nor defender activities cause unexpected problems in the operational or target environment. The White Cell is often tasked with:

Serving as referee between Red Team activities and defender responses during an engagement

- Establishing metrics for the engagement
- Coordinating activities on both sides to ensure engagement goals are achieved
- Providing the information required to conduct an efficient engagement
- Assisting with deconfliction activities between the Red Team and the defenders
- Scoring the engagement (if applicable)
- Providing a consolidated list of lessons learned obtained through observation during and after—action request immediately following the engagement

The White Cell is also responsible for correlating activities conducted by the Red Team with actions performed by the defenders (including times, systems, networks, team communications, etc.). This data is beneficial to the defenders as well as to the control group in identifying shortfalls in the security of the environment and defensive actions.

It is important to note that the White Cell is an observer and data correlator role, and not part of the target environment or engagement team. The White Cell should receive information from the defender but never deliver information to the defender. Any information provided to the defender must be routed through the Engagement or Exercise Control Group.

Engagement Control Group (ECG)

The Engagement (or Exercise) Control Group is ultimately responsible for all activities conducted during the engagement. This responsibility includes:

- Approving the engagement schedule, objectives, and directives
- Approving the Red Team objective targets for inclusion in engagement planning
- Establishing a time-coordinated blacklist for the environment (if required)
- Providing the environment information needed to construct scenarios that meet all objectives for the engagement
- Providing management and direction for the execution of the engagement
- Determining if, when, and what information should be provided to the defender during execution (a.k.a. injects)
- Determining when actions should be implemented as part of an engagement operational impact

Most often, the ECG is composed of one or two senior managers from the target environment (for example, a Chief Information Officer or Chief Operating Officer), one member from the Information Technology department of the organization, a White Cell liaison, and a Red Team liaison. Others can be added as required. All must be Trusted Agents. Some communities consolidate the ECG and White Cell into a single group with varying individual roles. When this occurs, an Engagement Control Director must be selected to interface with the Red Team and control the flow of information to the defenders.

Trusted Agent (TA)

A trusted agent is a member of the target organization who knows an engagement is underway. The Trusted Agent's primary role is to limit irreversible damage and risk to life, limb, eyesight, and equipment; however, they are more often used to prevent the defenders from causing unexpected self-inflicted damage. A TA has privileged and detailed knowledge of engagement activities, milestones, conditions, and the engagement status that would unduly bias or influence the actions of the environment staff and defenders. A Trusted Agent must protect all information from being provided to any party without the express approval of the ECG. Each engagement should establish a Trusted Agent Agreement that specifies to whom data can be delivered and under what approval process. Each TA must execute the agreement before receiving any information about the engagement.

Observers

If observers are required, their role is to document the actions and reactions of each cell during the execution phase of the engagement. They do not have knowledge of the engagement or scenario and do not provide information, suggestions, assistance, guidance, etc. for any cell; however, the observer may report potentially damaging actions to the white cell to ensure they are addressed.

Red Cell

The term red cell is borrowed from the military. It is commonly associated with a group that plays OPFOR (opposing force) during red vs. blue exercises. A red cell is the components that make up the offensive portion of a Red Team engagement. The red cell is typically comprised of Red Team leads and operators and is commonly referred to as Red Team instead of Red Cell.

Red Team Lead

A Red Team should have a lead for each engagement. The lead may perform the role of the action officer, the engagement lead, an operator, the customer interface, and, often, an analyst. In general, the Red Team lead:
- Provides overall direction and guidance for the team

- Provides information and research data for all laws, regulations, policies, programs, and operations
- Provides oversight for operational planning and execution
- Coordinates with each of the roles within the Red Team engagement
- Plans and manages the budget, personnel, and equipment
- Provides oversight for the team calendar
- Provides information related to engagements, capabilities, technology, and trends
- Provisions training and personnel development requirements
- Performs a budget analysis, including equipment and travel
- Identifies technical research and development directions

When planning or executing an engagement, the Red Team Lead:
- Oversees coordination with all stakeholders for the purpose of engagement execution
- Oversees training activities
- Is responsible for maintaining and coordinating logistics and the scheduling of the engagement space, time, and equipment
- Oversees compliance with all laws, regulations, policies, programs, and operations
- Is responsible for ensuring the accurate and timely completion of a final engagement report

Red Team Operator

Red Team operators are the individuals who execute the actions required for an engagement to meet the goals. Each Red Team operator complies with all Red Team policies and regulations under the direction of the Red Team Lead. In general, the operator:
- Executes engagement requirements as directed
- Complies with all laws, regulations, policies, programs, and Rules of Engagement
- Implements the team's operational methodology and TTPs
- Identifies and has input to target environment deficiencies

- Researches and develops new exploit and tests tools for functionality
- Performs Open Source Intelligence as required for the engagement
- Identifies and assesses actions that reveal system vulnerabilities and capabilities
- Assists the Red Team Lead in the development of the final engagement report
- Performs physical assessment support under the direction of Red Team Lead
- Executes operational impacts as approved by the ECG

Blue Cell

The blue cell is the opposite side of red. Is it all the components defending a target network. The blue cell is typically comprised of blue team members, defenders, internal staff, and an organization's management.

Engagement Relationships

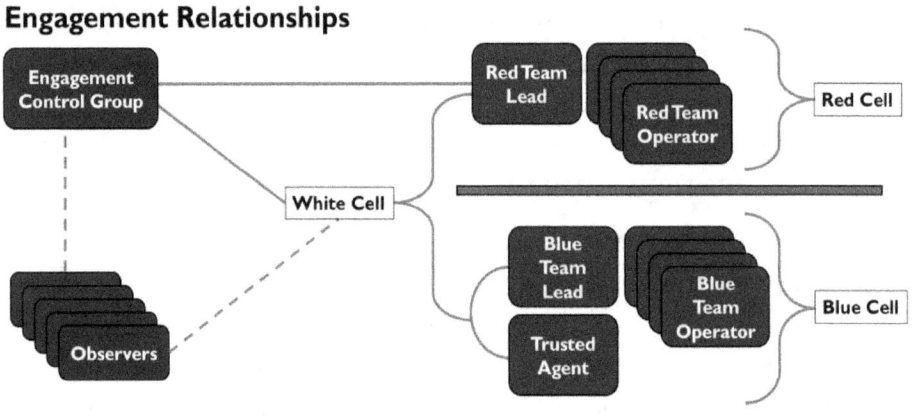

This diagram shows the relationship and communication paths among the different groups in an engagement. The red team lead maintains constant communication with the ECG and white cell. The blue team lead and trusted agents maintain communication with the white cell. The dashed line from the observers represents limited communications to the individuals overseeing an engagement.

Rules of Engagement (ROE)

The Rules of Engagement establish the responsibility, relationship, and guidelines between the Red Team, the network owner, the system owner, and any stakeholders required for engagement execution.

This document contains all agreed-upon rules for an engagement, should be a signed official agreement of all parties involved, is used as the formal agreement that authorizes the engagement actions, and should be treated as law. The ROE governs the entire process of a Red Team engagement and must be adhered to during the execution. Violation of the ROE can put a target organization or engagement operators at risk. The seriousness of the ROE must not be taken lightly. All parties must approve any deviation from the rules established in the ROE before execution.

ROE Document

The ROE documents the target information, approvals, threat implementation, activities, and issues required to staff, coordinate, and execute engagements within the target environment.

The main body of the ROE (often derived from a standing template) provides information on:
- The Red Team methodology
- A high-level description of the types of activities that may be executed
- The types of hardware and software that may be employed
- A recommended deconfliction process
- Levels of threat available (comparison)
- Roles and responsibilities of each functional group (ECG, White Cell, TA, etc.)

- The identification of and references to appropriate legal requirements (PCI, FERPA, HIPAA, HITEC, SOX, GLBA, etc.)
- A legal responsibility disclaimer (federally mandated requirements for the Red Team to report specific findings)

Information specific to each engagement should be documented in annexes to the ROE. At a minimum, ROE annexes should detail:

The Target of the Engagement
- Organization name
- Address
- Specific groups or divisions
- Organizational identifiers
- Senior management contact info

An Engagement Contact List (name, role, phone, email, office location)
- ECG personnel
- White Cell
- Trusted Agents
- Red Team Lead
- Red Tech Lead

Engagement Objectives
- Conditions
- Threat level
- Targeted objectives
- Targets of opportunity
- Measures of success/failure

Authorized Target Space
- Network
    - The IP boundaries of the event
    - Domains and workgroups

- - Specific off-limits areas and resources (e.g. non-target intellectual property file share)
  - Off-limits machines, networks, equipment, or applications (blacklist)
  - Maintenance windows
- Physical
  - Areas of the campus
  - Buildings
  - Offices
  - Off-limits areas (e.g., the emergency services sector of a medical complex)
  - Off-limits materials within the target space (e.g., sensitive documents or equipment)

Authorized Actions: Types of activities approved for the engagement
Restricted Actions: Types of activities restricted during the engagement (if any)

Approval Process

The process for requesting approval of additional activities during engagement execution

- Approval process
- Points of contact (name, role, phone, email, office location)
- Alternate POC

The ROE must be updated when the target space, authorized actions, objectives, or scope are changed. For instance, the original scope may be limited to computer network attacks. If physical attacks are planned, the ROE must be updated to reflect the additional activities and controls. The Red Team Lead will address suggestions or adjustments to the ROE. Each review must be provided to the originator. The final ROE must be signed by a Trusted Agent in senior management of the target environment.

Managing Risk

This section discusses risk (as a result of Red Team activities) to the target environment, NOT inherent vulnerabilities or weaknesses.

Risk management is the process of identifying, assessing, and controlling risks arising from engagement factors and making decisions that balance risk costs with target benefits. The objective of managing risk is not to eliminate all risk but to remove unnecessary risk.

The engagement planning process should identify and minimize any risks that may occur either directly or indirectly as a result of the Red Team's activities. The objective is to implement the efforts outlined in the ROE without causing any irreversible damage to the target environment. The ECG has overall responsibility for implementing risk management and accepting the risk to the target environment during the engagement. The Red Team Lead has responsibility for implementing risk management and accepting the risk guidelines into the team's objectives during the engagement. Before and throughout the event, the Red Team Lead may request the TA and ECG to assess all risks associated with current Red Team activities and vice versa.

Risk Management assists the engagement planning by:
- Conserving the limited resources used throughout an engagement
- Identifying potential risks early to avert this unwarranted risk
- Making an informed decision as to the course of action implementation (or alternate)
- Identifying feasible and effective control measures to ensure an engagement meets assessment goals without introducing unnecessary risk to the safety and health of the target
- Providing alternatives for objective or goal accomplishment when a risk is too high.

Risk Management does not:

- Limit the Red Team's ability to operate to the degree where engagement's goals can not be met
- Completely dissolve all risk (it manages risk)
- Mandate a decision on activity (it provides guidance to the ECG on mitigations or alternate decisions)
- Have the authority to violate the law even to support the successful execution of an engagement
- Eliminate requirements for SOP and TTP exercise

What does this mean in practical execution?

Every engagement must include risk management in planning and execution. Security testers and Red Team operators have been invited to play in someone else's playground. Care and consideration must be appropriately handled through risk management. Risk management does not mean risk elimination. The purpose is to identify risk early and develop a plan to handle situations where a pre-identified risk or unknown risk is realized.

The risk management process:
1. Identify potential issues, conflicts, or hazards (life, limb, eyesight, equipment, and production)
2. Assess each to determine the direct impact to the target environment
3. Develop controls designed to mitigate risks
4. Make a risk decision
5. Implement controls
6. Identify residual risk (alter controls until the residual risk is acceptable or cannot be further reduced)
7. Continually assess risk

Threat Planning

A major factor of the engagement is the threat type and characteristics the Red Team must portray. This is achieved through threat planning. The end state of threat planning is an ability to represent the threat as closely as possible and to advise the target of implications to the target environment. Effective planning through the construction of TTPs, profiles, and scenarios significantly improves the Red Team's ability to ensure the engagement identifies potential threat vectors and assists defensive operations with identifying gaps in processes, procedures, toolsets, and training.

The level and depth of threat planning are driven by goals and are different on every engagement. At a minimum, threat planning should include the use of threat TTPs specifically required to achieve a goal and optionally the characteristics of specific threat actors or threat groups. Consider the following when planning how a threat will be used during an engagement.

- Threat landscape
    - What are the target's characteristics?
    - What specific TTPs will be required to operate in that environment?
- Threat to the target environment
    - What are the current threats to an environment identified through OSINT?
    - What are the current threat concerns of the customer, current issue, or previous events?
- Real-world examples of threats
    - What current or prior threats are of concern?
- Threat in scenario or engagement conditions
    - How will the engagement scenario impact the threat landscape?
- Level of threat capability the team will attempt to emulate

- Is the threat capability or level (simple to advanced) important in the engagement scenario?

A factor Red Team leaders must consider is the realism of the threat. While some organizations may intentionally decide not to unleash the full capabilities of the threat (e.g., due to the level of target audience aptitude or environmental constraints), most Red Teams select attack types and strategies to simulate realistic threats. Exploitation for exploitation's sake or a show of Red Team strength is not appropriate and will not provide meaningful results. Defining threat-based attacks will provide a viable mechanism for training the target audience and strengthening the target environment. The Red Team Lead should carefully weigh the different options in the context of the engagement. This list will then form the basis of the emerging engagement strategy.

Threat intelligence provides information for analysis, the creation of a threat profile, and characterization of the threat. A significant factor in the construction of this characterization is the consideration of the threat's perspective, which can be from inside the target, outside the target, or having limited access to the target. This profile and characterization information is used to create threat scenarios. Threat intelligence also feeds the replication of a threat's intent, capabilities, and TTPs. These can be used to classify and characterize a threat.

Intent

The intent is the "why" in threat operations. The threat's intent may vary greatly depending upon the target, the sensitivity and value of the target's information, and the desired impacts on both the target and the threat. A threat's intent is based on the specifics of an engagement.

A threat may simply want to gather target information. This information is typically something classified as confidential, proprietary, or intellectual property, and if lost, would be detrimental to an organization. For example, stolen data could be provided to competitors to build and release in time with or ahead of the target.

The intent may be to insert faulty or malicious code into the target's current software project. This code could cause failure or security vulnerabilities at software release. Manipulation scenarios are an excellent choice to support a supply chain attack scenario.

The threat may want to impact the target's sales and possibly cause a business failure by releasing target information to the public.

Intent that directly impacts an organization should be considered during planning over intent that simply identifies technical flaws.

Capabilities

Capabilities are simply a threat's ability to perform actions given the current funding, technical knowledge and skill, and target knowledge. A common issue observed in many different industries is the underestimation of a threat's capability. It is essential to note that information, tools, scripts, designs, training, etc. available to most information technology and security professionals are also available to the threat.

TTPs

TTPs are the "how" in threat operations. TTPs are dependent upon the threat's intent and capabilities. Understanding threat TTPs are extremely useful to both the Red and the Blue Team as the use and understanding of TTP's is one of the most effective ways to classify and characterize threats by actions.

Consider these questions when planning threat TTP's
(Don't forget to consider the red team's ability to implement these)

- What is the threat's preferred method of gaining initial access? Web misconfigurations? Known vulnerabilities? Phishing?
- Are there trends in the Indicators of Compromise (IOCs)? Things such as file locations, filenames, system calls, anomalous traffic, etc.
- How does the threat perform operations and maintenance against a target? Memory resident? Binaries? Python? WMI? PowerShell? VBS?
- How does the Command and Control (C2) operate? Using what protocols?
- Is persistence established? What are the threat's preferred methods?
- Does the threat have a standard or common motive and intent?

A Red Team's analysis of a threat's intent, capabilities, and TTPs provides the information required to create the threat profile. This profile enables the threat characterization used for targeted reviews, assessments, training, and exercises.

Threat Profile

Planning is vital to emulate a threat or their TTPs. Without a plan, modeling a sophisticated actor can become extremely difficult, time-consuming, and costly. Too often, Red Teams attempt to emulate a highly advanced actor, such as "APT group X" or "nation state" with little to no time or budget. Sophisticated actors have time, money, and resources to build and develop custom tools, exploits, or techniques. This understanding may seem obvious, but it is important to remember that a Red Team charged with emulating a specific actor is not that actor. The team may not have the time or budget needed to emulate a threat perfectly. However, a threat can be emulated just enough to stay within a reasonable budget, as well as the amount of time, and effort needed to model a threat's core components.

The Red Team should be helping personnel understand how a specific threat impacts their organization. To facilitate this practice, a threat profile is used to establish the rules as to how a Red Team will act and operate. These rules serve as a roadmap for a Red Team by guiding how and what type of actions should be performed. Even during an in-depth Red Team engagement, a threat profile should be created to describe the threat and their TTPs.

We've discussed TTPs, but until this point, we haven't provided a means to use them to support an engagement. Let's start by explaining TTP's through the MITRE ATT&CK framework. MITRE's Adversarial Tactics, Techniques, and Common Knowledge (ATT&CK™) is a curated knowledge base and model for cyber threat behavior, reflecting the various phases of a threat's lifecycle and the platforms they are known to target. ATT&CK is useful for understanding security risk against known threat behavior, for planning security improvements, and verifying defenses work as expected. ATT&CK is split into Tactics, Techniques, and Procedures. Tactics are the tactical goals a threat may use during an operation. Techniques describe the actions threats take to achieve their objectives. Procedures are the technical steps required to perform an action. This framework provides a classification of all threat actions regardless of the underlying vulnerabilities.

Red teams can emulate realistic TTPs through research and experience, but much of this information has been compiled in ATT&CK. ATT&CK can be thought of like a menu of TTPs. Red teams can use this to ensure they have a valid threat profile with a comprehensive set of threat TTPs, and blue teams can use this to build a scorecard of how well they can defend against the various TTPs.

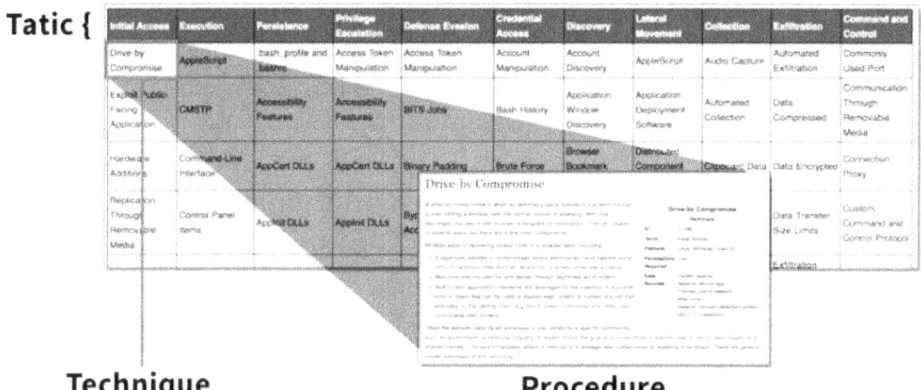

MITRE ATT&CK Tactics

Initial Access
The initial access tactic represents the vectors adversaries use to gain an initial foothold within a network.

Execution
The execution tactic represents techniques that result in execution of threat-controlled code on a local or remote system. This tactic is often used in conjunction with initial access as a means of executing code once access is obtained, and lateral movement to expand access to remote systems on a network.

Persistence
Persistence is any access, action, or configuration change to a system that gives a threat a persistent presence on that system. Adversaries will often need to maintain access to systems through interruptions such as system restarts, loss of credentials, or other failures that would require a remote access tool to restart or alternate backdoor for them to regain access.

Privilege escalation

Privilege escalation is the result of actions that allows a threat to obtain a higher level of permissions on a system or network. Certain tools or actions require a higher level of privilege to work and are likely necessary at many points throughout an operation. Adversaries can enter a system with unprivileged access and must take advantage of a system weakness to obtain local or domain administrator or SYSTEM/root level privileges. A user account with administrator-like access can also be used. User accounts with permissions to access specific systems (or perform specific functions necessary for adversaries to achieve their objective) may also be considered an escalation of privilege.

Defense evasion
Defense evasion consists of techniques a threat may use to evade detection or avoid other defenses. Sometimes these actions are the same as or variations of techniques in other categories that have the added benefit of subverting a particular defense or mitigation. Defense evasion may be considered a set of attributes the threat applies to all other phases of the operation.

Credential access
Credential access represents techniques resulting in access to or control over system, domain, or service credentials that are used within an enterprise environment. Adversaries will likely attempt to obtain legitimate credentials from users or administrator accounts (local system administrator or domain users with administrator access) to use within the network. This allows the threat to assume the identity of the account, with all of that account's permissions on the system and network, and makes it harder for defenders to detect the threat. With sufficient access within a network, a threat can create accounts for later use within the environment.

Discovery
Discovery consists of techniques that allow the threat to gain knowledge about the system and internal network. When adversaries gain access to a

new system, they must orient themselves to what they now have control of and what benefits operating from that system give to their current objective or overall goals during the intrusion. The operating system provides many native tools that aid in this post-compromise information-gathering phase.

Lateral movement
Lateral movement consists of techniques that enable a threat to access and control remote systems on a network and could, but does not necessarily, include execution of tools on remote systems. The lateral movement techniques could allow a threat to gather information from a system without needing additional tools, such as a remote access tool.

Collection
Collection consists of techniques used to identify and gather information, such as sensitive files, from a target network prior to exfiltration. This category also covers locations on a system or network where the threat may look for information to exfiltrate.

Exfiltration
Exfiltration refers to techniques and attributes that result or aid in the threat removing files and information from a target network. This category also covers locations on a system or network where the threat may look for information to exfiltrate.

Command and Control
The command and control tactic represents how adversaries communicate with systems under their control within a target network. There are many ways a threat can establish command and control, with various levels of covertness, depending on system configuration and network topology. Due to the wide degree of variation available to the threat at the network level, only the most common factors were used to describe the differences in command and control. There are still a great many specific techniques within the documented methods, largely due to how easy it is to define

new protocols and use existing, legitimate protocols and network services for communication.

Creating a Threat Profile by Decomposing a Threat

Threat profiles can be built by decomposing existing threats into core components then recomposing them into profiles a Red Team can use to describe and execute a Red Team engagement.

The Management Challenge

When a Red Team is asked to perform threat emulation of a specific actor, the limits of budget, time, and effort can easily be pushed to the edge.

Strong Red Team leadership is required to bridge the gap of realism and effectiveness when emulating a threat. Breaking down a threat into its components and choosing those items that best exercise the engagement's goals provides leadership a roadmap of how the threat will be accurately represented. In this way, a threat can be emulated within a budget, time, and resource-constrained environment.

Creating a threat profile is a great way of establishing the rules as to how a Red Team will act and operate. These act as a roadmap for a Red Team by providing guidance on how and what type of actions should be performed. They help all sides (Red and Blue) ensure the Red Team is emulating the correct threat. Remember, a Red Team engagement is not an all-out hack fest. In many cases, a Red Team is helping personnel understand how a specific threat impacts an organization. Even during an in-depth, full-scale Red Team engagement, a threat profile should be created. It helps describe the threat and their TTPs. This material is ideal for setting the scenario, threading a threat's story, and can immensely improve the final report.

Threat Profile Example (Simplified)

Category	Description
Description	General mid-tiered threat that uses common offensive tools and techniques.
Goal and Intent	Exist in the network to enumerate systems and information in order to maintain Command and Control to support future attacks.
Key IOCs	Cobalt Strike HTTPS beacon on TCP 443, Payload: c:\programdata\microsoft\iexplore.exe, Timestamp: 7/13/2009 10:04 PM, MD5: a7705501c5e216b56cf49dcf540184d0
C2 Overview	HTTPS on port 443 Cobalt Strike Beacon with a five-minute callback time. Calling directly to threat-owned domains. TTPs (Enumeration, Delivery, Lateral Movement, Privilege Escalation, etc.) Assumed Breach Model, no initial delivery via exploitation. POST-exploitation via Cobalt Strike commands. Enumeration and lateral movement via Cobalt Strike and native Windows commands. Privilege escalation limited and determined POST-exploitation.
Exploitation	Assumed Breach Model, no exploitation.
Persistence	User-level persistence using Microsoft Outlook rule triggered by specific email.

The above is a simplified example profile from an actual Red Team engagement. This engagement was one part of a series of assessments designed to test a Blue Team's capability of detecting and profiling a threat. It required the use of defined and specific TTPs. This is the heart of threat emulation. Defining the profile allowed all parties to be on the same page. At the end of the assessment, the profile was shared with the Blue Team members to assist the discovery anything that may have been missed. This provided defenders with the information needed to identify any gaps in their TTPs, which greatly helped them improve.

The process of decomposing a threat involves:
1. Research of existing threat
2. Breaking down the key elements of a threat profile. (description, goal and intent, key IOCs, C2 overview, exploitation, and persistence)
3. Recomposing the threat in the form of a profile using information learned and filling gaps with alternate TTPs (MITRE ATT&CK is a great source to help fill these gaps)

Threat Profile Usage

Threat profiles typically support the engagement story and are used to describe the technical aspects of a single C2 channel. A single threat profile is used for each C2 channel.

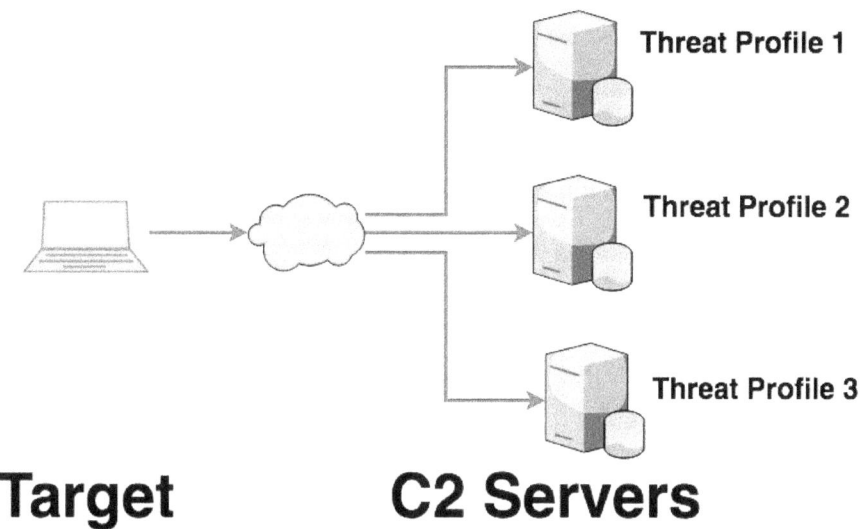

At the end of this chapter, you will have the opportunity to work through a threat profile exercise. Let's examine an example of a real attack to illustrate the concept of a threat profile.

A review of a blackhat's tradecraft

This real-world attack will provide context and understanding of how an attack may occur. As you read through the summary, think about how you could use this in planning and scoping a red team engagement.

How HackingTeam Got Hacked

Phineas Fisher, a.k.a. Hack Back!, claims responsibility for the Hacking Team attack and release of documents. The documents were released to WikiLeaks on July 8, 2015. In April 2016, Phineas Fisher published a report explaining how the Hacking Team attack was accomplished. It was first written in Spanish and later translated into English.

Tweet Sent from HT's Twitter account after it was controlled by Phineas Fisher

Hacking Team, an Italian company, is known for selling intrusion and surveillance software to governments, law enforcement agencies, and corporations. We will not focus on whether you agree with their practices or not. What is interesting here is the opportunity to review a black hat's Tradecraft. Why? A Red Team may need to defend their position on how and why they acted in a certain way. It is common for target organizations to claim that specific techniques are not real or that a threat "would not do that". This article is a great reference to use in threat emulation. The TTPs described are not only are useful in performing an engagement but can help confirm that a Red Team's actions are threat faithful. Threat faithful engagements that closely mimic a realistic threat, are very believable and a great way to demonstrate practical adversarial activity.

For more detailed information on this attack, read the following:
1. Hack Back!, http://pastebin.com/raw/0SNSvyjJ.
2. Hacking Team, https://wikileaks.org/hackingteam/emails/.
3. Hacking Team, https://en.wikipedia.org/wiki/Hacking_Team.
4. .Hack Back!, http://pastebin.com/raw/GPSHF04A.
5. Full English translation of Phineas Fisher's account of how he took down HackingTeam, https://www.reddit.com/r/netsec/comments/4f3e6p/full_english_translation_of_phineas_fishers/d25qbci/.
6. https://www.vice.com/en_us/article/3k9zzk/hacking-team-hacker-phineas-fisher-has-gotten-away-with-it

How the Hack[12] Went Down

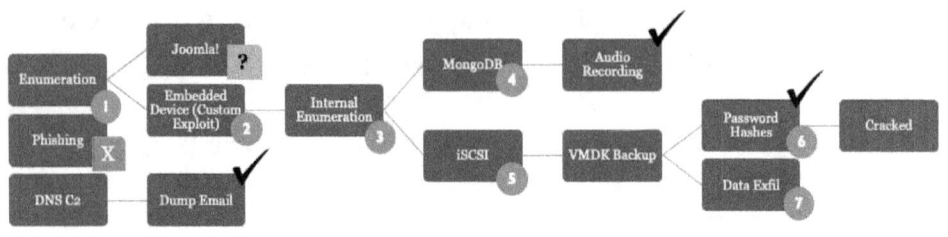

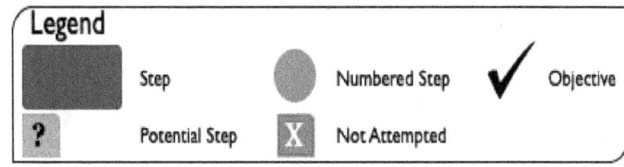

Attack Diagram of Hacking Team highlighting major steps

Fisher started by analyzing the target. Fisher recognized that spear-phishing was risky. *"I didn't want to try to spear phish Hacking Team, as their whole business is helping governments spear phish their opponents, so they'd be much more likely to recognize and investigate a spear phishing attempt."* Early analysis showed the Hacking Team's network appeared to be hardened and to have a small attack surface. Initial analysis revealed an updated version of Joomla!, a mail server, a couple of routers, a VPN appliance, and a spam filter. Gaining initial access was not straightforward. Attacking Joomla! with an exploit or zero-day, or attacking an embedded device with a yet to be determined path seemed the best option for initial access. After a few weeks of development, a successful zero-day exploit was created for an unnamed embedded device. This zero-day provided root access to the device and was used as the initial entry point. Internal enumeration was

---

[12] "How Hacking Team got hacked | Ars Technica." 19 Apr. 2016, https://arstechnica.com/information-technology/2016/04/how-hacking-team-got-hacked-phineas-phisher/.

performed after this initial access. The enumeration revealed a MongoDB instance that required no authentication. This database provided access to an audio recording that was part of an audio spying application. These recordings were interesting but not detrimental. Fisher wanted to damage this company and expose them for involvement is something more severe than selling spying software. Further exploration led to the identification of this damaging information. The significant data was found in an unsecured iSCSI server that contained backup VMware .vmdk files and other beneficial information. Eventually, administrative level password hashes were dumped from the backups. Many of the administrative password hashes were successfully cracked. These passwords allowed access to other systems including an email server. PowerShell was used to access and download current emails. More than 1 million emails were downloaded.

In total, Phineas Fisher was in the Hacking Team network for about six weeks and spent about 100 hours moving and stealing data. The attack was primarily politically motivated.

This example is almost identical to that of a Red Team engagement.
An intelligent actor analyzed a target to determine the best path forward, crafted a custom attack, elevated privileges, identified information, and stole sensitive data.

Additional References:
1. How Hacking Team got hacked, http://arstechnica.com/security/2016/04/how-hacking-team-got-hacked-phineas-phisher/.
2. The Vigilante Who Hacked Hacking Team Explains How He Did It, http://motherboard.vice.com/read/the-vigilante-who-hacked-hacking-team-explains-how-he-did-it.

Analyzing the TTPs described in the Hacking Team attack is a great way to understand how a real threat attacks a target. Analysis can be used to validate TTPs plans or to learn new techniques that can be applied to future engagements. Although this was an illegal attack against a company, it provided useful insights into how a threat thinks and acts.

TTPs Used in the Hacking Team Attack

Hacktivist	Politically motivated	Watch and listen	Perform internal enumeration.
Know your target	Don't spear phish a company that specializes in spear phishing.	Know a range of technologies	Windows domains, NoSQL DB, iSCSI, etc.
Maintain good OPSEC	Don't directly connect to target systems. Use a pivot and redirectors.	Escalate privileges	Gain cleartext credentials to enable capabilities.
C2	Domains for DNS C2,;stable C2 servers for callbacks and loot storage; hacked servers for pivots, scans, etc. Consider burnable.	Steal email	Download email using PowerShell scripts and smbclient.
Enumeration	Google, Whois, controlled port scanning from burnable IP space.	Lateral movement	Psexec, WMI, PSRemoting, scheduled tasks, GPO.
Exploit once and move on	Use, exploit once, and move to other backdoors. Minimize exposure through exploitation.	Persistence	Execute in RAM in high uptime servers.
		Length	~ Six weeks and 100 hours.
Be prepared	Have post-exploitation tools and scripts ready.	http://pastebin.com/0SNSvyjJ	

A simple threat profile can be developed to provide a general description of the threat using the HackingTeam attack.

Characterizing the HT Attack Threat Profile

Category	Description
Description	Politically motivated hacktivist capable of developing zero days.
Goal and Intent	Capture sensitive information about HackingTeam to expose, defame, and otherwise cause harm to the target.
Key IOCs	DNS memory-resident C2 agents.
C2 Overview	DNS C2, "burnable" C2 for more aggressive scans and enumeration.
TTPs (Enumeration, Delivery, Lateral Movement, Privilege Escalation, etc.)	Enumeration via Open Source Intelligence gathering. Delivery via custom attacks and memory-resident tools. Lateral movement specific to each target's ports/services (Psexec, WMI, PSRemoting, scheduled tasks, GPO). Privilege escalation limited and determined POST-exploitation.
Exploitation	Custom exploits and attacks.
Persistence	Exist in RAM on high uptime systems.

Questions to consider regarding Red Team scoping.

1) Could your Red Team perform these actions?

    If not, consider your team's ability to emulate these actions and possibly enhancing with training or internal development.

2) Do you have access to zero-days? If not, how would you emulate this sort of attack?

    Many teams do not have zero-days or time allocated to develop them. Consider using white carded scenarios to emulate these types of attacks.

3) This attack took six weeks, 100+ hours, and a single person to complete. This is a great metric for scope duration. Could your team do the same?

    Does your team have the necessary skills, knowledge, abilities, tools, TTPs, etc. to perform within the same timeframe? Consider adjusting your timeline and hour allocation to accommodate your team's capabilities.

4) Would you scope an engagement with the same staff and time parameters?

    Team's should not operate alone. No matter what issue a team has with staffing or budget, an engagement should have at least twice this staffing. As for time, six weeks may be longer than possible. If so, consider what is in or out of scope. Consider using the assumed breach model to help utilize resources efficiently.

Threat Perspective

As briefly mentioned earlier, a Threat's Perspective is the threat's initial point of view. This perspective is used to build and shape a threat profile or scenario. A threat's perspective may be that of an outsider, nearsider, or insider.

Outsider	
An entity that has no legitimate access to specific software, systems, and networks. An outsider is anyone outside an organization.	An example would be a competitor's employee who would not have authorized physical or digital access to any systems, network, software, or hardware.
Nearsider	
An entity that has no legitimate access to specific software, systems, and networks but may have physical access to buildings and equipment or access to systems that integrate with target assets	An example would be janitorial staff. They would not likely have authorized digital access to any systems or networks, but may have physical access to buildings, communication facilities, systems, networks, etc.
Insider	
An entity that has legitimate access to specific software, systems, and networks and has physical access to buildings and equipment	An example of a malicious insider is a rogue system administrator who has authorized, privileged access and willingly removes information from target assets or modifies target assets to cause failure

	An example of a non-malicious insider is an employee on the sales staff who has authorized access to the systems, networks, software, and hardware required to perform sales. The individual may be an unknowing target during initial access

There are several methods used to gain access to a target system. Initial access is debated too often during Red Team planning. Using a diagram like the one below during planning can help you decide a starting point based on goals. Each dot represents a potential starting point. The type of access needed at each point is different. Build this into the Red Team plan. The process of deciding the threat perspective is fundamental. The scenario and engagement goals drive this decision. For example, the goals of an engagement include measuring the ability for security operations to identify and respond to a threat moving through the company's network. The effective use of resources would be to start the engagement somewhere inside this network. Forcing a team to establish access from outside the network could waste the limited engagement time on steps that do not directly support engagement goals.

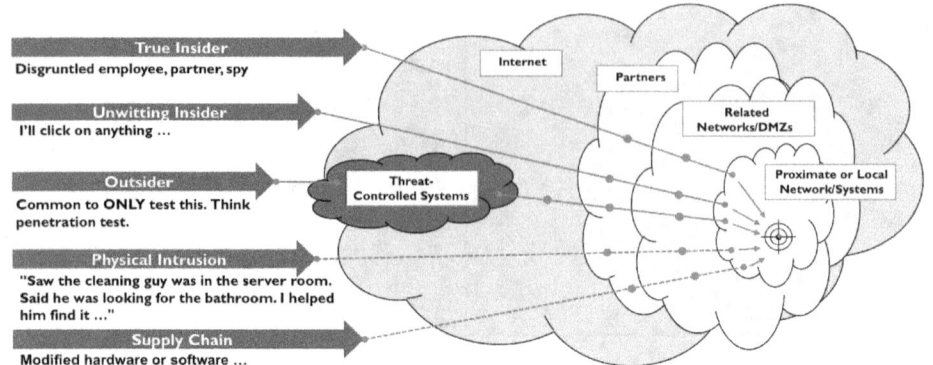

> **How to use this diagram in planning**
>
> This diagram can be used to help plan starting points based on the threat perspective. Don't begin with the assumption that all engagements must start from the outside. Discuss the goals of the engagement along with the desired scenario. Suggest a few points on the diagram that best illustrates the scenario. Discuss how this point represents the engagement scenario. Use the point that will best lead to the achievement of engagement goals.

Threat Scenario

A core aspect of Red Teaming is threat scenarios. Scenarios provide insight into how a defensive solution will perform and conform to the processes, procedures, policies, activities, personnel, organizations, environment, threats, constraints, assumptions, and support involved in the security mission. Scenarios generally describe the role of the threat, how it will interact with the systems and networks within the target environment, and elicits real-world truth of how essential internal practices are employed. In short, it answers how the target's security operations would dynamically perform an action to deliver results, outputs, or prove capability.

A Red Team engagement driven by a specific scenario narrows the focus to a particular area. This allows a concept to be explored at a deeper level. Scenarios allow a specific threat to be emulated and exposed to a target organization. A scenario-based approach can offer additional value over standard penetration testing or vulnerability assessments. The observations and understanding of how a specific threat can impact an organization provide the knowledge needed to efficiently allocate the limited time, money, and resources of an organization to best defend its assets.

To simplify, Red Teams explore the "threat story." A scenario provides the script for that story and drives how a Red Team emulates a threat. A Red Team uses the plot to shape their actions and develop their TTPs. All of these aspects combined create a comprehensive threat scenario.

How is this used in practice? Perhaps a target learns of a new type of malware through a threat intelligence feed. The malware is actively attacking the mobile applications of other, similar organizations. The organization can use a Red Team to design and emulate a specific scenario using the TTPs of the malware. Using threat intelligence reports or malware analysis reports, a Red Team can develop custom code or simulations that mirror the actions of the malware. Scenarios allow the institution to perform a scenario-based Red Team assessment to measure how well its systems will stand up to an attack from the new malware and potentially how it would perform against similar actions of unknown malware.

Designing scenarios can be challenging. It is common to select a scenario model that will not enable a Red Team to successfully achieve their goals in the time limits of an engagement. Remember that Red Teams are not finding flaws or vulnerabilities as in a penetration test but stimulating and performing impacts against an organization to measure security operations as a whole.

Threat Emulation

Threat Emulation is the process of mimicking the TTPs of a specific threat. A Red Team performs threat emulation by acting as a representative threat. Threats of any variety can be emulated. This can include:
- Zero-day or custom attacks
- Script kiddie to advanced threat
- Emulation of specific threat tools or techniques (botnets, DDOS, ransomware, specific malware, APT, etc.)

Scenario-driven assessments are typically driven by the emulation of some level of threat. This may be a specific threat, such as the Havex trojan used by Energetic Bear / Crouching Yeti / Dragonfly, or a general threat, such as a simple Command and Control botnet. Regardless of the scenario, the TTPs outlined drive the rules a Red Team must follow to perform an engagement. When a threat emulation scenario is being designed, that threat's key components should be defined. While it can be difficult to emulate a specific threat in detail, this does not mean the threat cannot be emulated, or there is no value in attempting to do so. A Red Team should focus on following a threat's key components and use its own TTPs to fill in the gaps. A Red Team is not the original designer or author of a threat, but is a highly skilled and capable group that can (and should) reinforce an emulated threat's TTPs with its own developed Tradecraft and processes. In this way, the Red Team can model a threat actor in a way that supports the goals of a threat-based scenario.

The biggest challenge in threat emulation is executing to a level where an analyst believes the threat is real. Approaches may include the use of known bad malware, developing custom malware that models a threat, using tools that generate the Indicators of Compromise (IOCs) of a known threat, or simply using system and network native tools and commands. Effective planning and determining the critical components of a threat will lead to a better threat emulation design.

Scenario Models

As stated earlier, it is common to select a scenario model that will not enable a Red Team to successfully achieve their goals within the time limits of an engagement. When selecting a scenario model, choose it based on what operational impacts should be measured. These models only help design a scenario. The execution of a scenario may be adjusted during an engagement. Being flexible and prepared to make adjustments is critical. If a Red Team is successful too quickly, observations may not be valuable. If a Red Team is stopped too soon, an organization may not get exposure to the desired impact. Selecting the right model will help ensure the right balance.

What does "scenario model" actually mean? Threat Emulation Scenario Models include Full Engagement Model, Assumed Breach Model, and Custom Scenario Model.

Full Engagement Model

The Full Engagement Model is a complete, end-to-end emulation of a threat and is the most common model desired by organizations. Think of this as the no-holds-barred engagement (although there are always holds barred). This model attempts to emulate a threat starting on day one and working until a final goal is reached.

A Full Engagement Model begins with the threat outside an organization. The threat must perform Open Source Intelligence (OSINT), reconnaissance, and enumeration to determine a path into the network. Once inside a network, the Red Team will continue to execute its plan using

its TTPs. This will continue until the Red Team is stopped or completes its goal. Characteristics of the Full Engagement Model:
- Begins on day 1 of adversarial activity
- Red Team must perform all phases (Get In, Stay In, and Act; to be discussed further in the text)
- Typically longer than other engagement types, as adequate time is needed to perform all phases
- Red Team must be able to get in or have a backup "white carding" plan
- With condensed execution timelines, it is common for time to run out before operational impacts can be executed
- Contingency plans must be made to ensure that required impacts are executed

Assumed Breach Model

The Assumed Breach Model assumes a threat has some level of access to a target at the initiation of the engagement. This model is arguably the most beneficial of all the models. The threat is assumed to have some level of access to a target before beginning. This starts a scenario much further into the attack timeline. Assuming someone can breach a network is often argued by less mature organizations who assume Red Teams must prove they can "get in" before beginning. When is this proof important? It is important ONLY if measuring the ability a threat has to "get in" is important. If this is not a key goal, using the Assumed Breach Model will save time, effort, and money; and will free the Red Team to explore higher impact goals. Characteristics of the Assumed Breach Model:
- Begins after a threat has breached an organization
- Red Team focuses on the Stay In and Act phases
- More efficient use of limited resources (time, money, and staff)
- Requires providing access to the Red Team. This is commonly done by launching a Red Team's malware, providing access to a specific asset, or providing passwords
- Operational impacts and goals must still be achieved

> **Consider This**
>
> **Assuming a breach can lead to disbelief in the results.**
> All too often, defensive staff and even senior managers attempt to downplay legitimate Red Team activities. With the assumed breach, more immature organizations may attempt to do so by hinging an activity's success to being "provided access to the system or network" rather than recognize the lessons learned by understanding how the defending team was able to execute its defensive strategies.

Custom Breach Model

Custom breach models allow the Red Team to design scenarios that enable the test or measurement of specific areas of concern to the target. A Custom Engagement Model:

- May start at any point in a threat cycle
- Focuses on any of the phases as designed by the goals and objectives
- Is highly efficient where limited staff, time, and funds are available
- Is nearly always announced and coordinated with real-time interaction

The Red Team should most often use an *Assume Breach* strategy. This strategy was made popular by Microsoft and is admittedly more philosophy than deduction. Reactively waiting for evidence of a breach causes companies to reveal not only that they have been compromised but that they have been compromised for years.

Indicators of Compromise

Although it is commonly thought that adversaries can clean up after themselves, it is almost impossible to remove all evidence. A good security operations team has the potential to find even the most advanced

adversaries. Evidence is always left behind. Indicators of Compromise (IOCs) are artifacts (bits of information) that identify or describe threat actions. An IOC can be anything used to identify a threat action including, but not limited to:
- Unusual network traffic
- Unusual user activity
- Geographic-specific connections
- Increased network traffic
- Increased database reads
- Unusual file changes or modifications
- Registry changes or modifications
- Specific naming or usage conventions
- Identifying actions or action attempts
- Signs of DOS/DDOS

Most security organizations rely on some trigger to take action. Systems such as network sensors, security sensors, or even end-users typically trigger an investigation of "strange" behavior. When a security team responds to a trigger, they are challenged to test their ability to leverage IOCs to identify, contain, and eradicate a threat. This play between Red and Blue generating and identifying IOCs is at the heart of Red Teaming. In order to replicate a malicious actor, a Red Team must understand a threat's TTPs. These TTPs are emulated by controlling the "when" and "how", as well as the type of IOC generated or left behind. Given this concept, Red Team Operators must know what indicators are made by a tool or action. If those IOCs are acceptable, they can proceed. If the IOCs are not acceptable, and the action is performed, there is a significant risk of exposing the Red Team before planned expectations. Not only is the management of an IOC necessary for threat emulation, but an IOC can get you caught when the timing is not appropriate and may also put an entire engagement at risk if not controlled and managed.

Controlling Tools

In order to control IOCs, a robust set of TTPs must exist. Part of these TTPs are tools that will support a Red Team's capability. The tools must not only provide capability but also must be understood. This is often done through tool usage and modification. Tools usage and modification should be built into a standard attack platform. If the platform is managed and maintained, a common baseline is ready for use. As a general rule, a Red Team should:

- Know the tools used, how they operate, and what actions are conducted
- Recompile tools (rename functions; remove help, comments, and unused code/strings; etc.)
- Control User-Agents
- Understand which IOCs are generated by an action
- Blend in until timing is appropriate

The following are common indicators and just a small example to help think about the indicators that must be controlled.

User Agents – User-Agent strings can be a dead giveaway for tools
- For example, the SQL injection tool SQLMAP has a default User-Agent string that includes the word sqlmap sqlmap/1.0-dev-xxxxxxx (http://sqlmap.org) This is very common.

Binaries may have signatures that can be detected
- Modification and recompiling may be necessary to change the signature
- The likelihood of Antivirus detection may be decreased by removing comments and other user output before compiling

> **Focus Point**
>
> The end state of threat planning is an ability to portray the threat as closely as possible to enable the ability to advise the target of implications to the target environment.

Engagement Concepts

Red Team engagements can move through several complex and detailed steps during execution but using three simple phases helps keep the focus on goals. Although Red Teaming is offensively focused, it is ultimately used as a tool to improve security. Red Teaming is executed in three phases directly related to areas of defense than can be tested and measured against a threat. It is common for security operations to focus a tremendous amount of time and energy on preventive controls to "keep the threat out." Prevention is important; however, 100% prevention is not feasible. An organization should understand potential impacts if a threat is successful.

Execution Phases

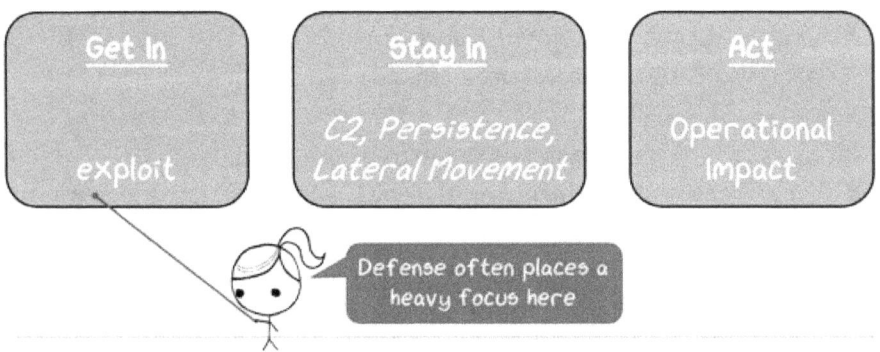

At a high level, a Red Team must move through these three phases to complete an engagement.

Get In - Gain access to a network. The Red Team must have access to their target. Access can be through a legitimate compromise or access is directly granted as part of an assumed breach scenario, such as an insider threat scenario.

> Can an organization detect a threat gaining access to its network?

Stay In - Establish persistence or a permanent presence. Red Team engagements are typically longer than other types of tests. A Red Team usually establishes persistence or a permanent presence in order to survive the duration of the engagement.

> Can an organization detect or prevent a threat from living in its network?

Act - Finally, a Red Team performs operational impacts against the target

> What impacts can a threat perform based on the capabilities it gained during Get In and Stay In?

Phase Mapping

Most penetration testing frameworks are broken down into individual phases that focus on vulnerability identification and exploitation. The Red Team methodology categorizes many of the same actions into only three distinct phases with a focus on the impacts caused to the target environment. Several examples of this categorization have been provided below.

Methodology

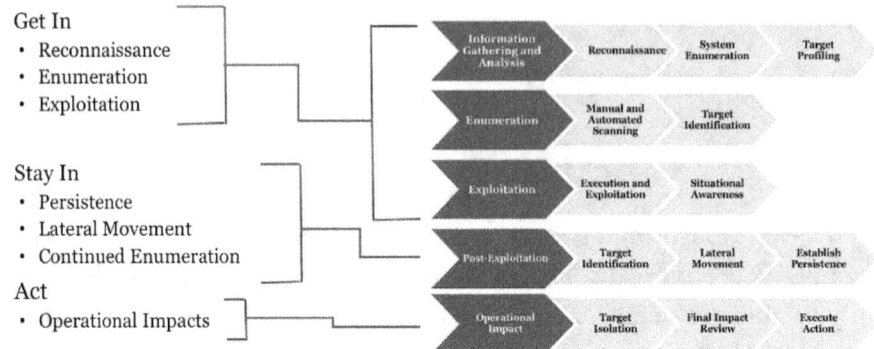

- Get In
  - Reconnaissance
  - Enumeration
  - Exploitation
- Stay In
  - Persistence
  - Lateral Movement
  - Continued Enumeration
- Act
  - Operational Impacts

GET IN

Reconnaissance
- Perform Open Source Intelligence (OSINT) against the target.
- Search using open, unauthenticated sources:
    - Target websites
    - Social media
    - Search engines
    - Public code repositories
    - Alternate target sites

External enumeration
- Identify external assets:
    - Perform a reverse DNS scan to identify registered hosts
    - Identify URLs and other external touch points from the scan and OSINT
- Evaluate the web presence:
    - Browse as a normal user through a web proxy to capture intelligence and understanding
    - Identify known vulnerabilities and vulnerable conditions
    - Do not send attack code at this time

90

- Execution and exploitation
    - Attempt to exploit targets based on current knowledge
    - Perform situational awareness on the target
    - Attempt local privilege elevation
    - Attempt domain or other system-level privilege elevation

STAY IN

Post-exploitation
- Continue internal and domain enumeration
- Identify domain users/groups/memberships
- Identify the IP space
- Identify file shares
- Establish persistence
- Use the persistence plan to place agents on target systems
- Move laterally

ACT

Operational Impacts
- Perform a realistic simulation against target systems
- Does not need to be highly complex
- Does not need to leverage known or traditional vulnerabilities
- Does not always require administrative (local/domain) privileges
- Does require an actual impact to the target environment
- Does require input from the ECG and TA
- Does require notification to the ECG and TA when the operational impact is executed
    - Avoids unwanted (and possibly catastrophic) defensive actions
- Does need to exercise at least one of the target's detection, incident response, continuity, and recovery plans and procedures

Operational impacts are a key distinguisher for Red Teaming engagements vs. other types of tests

Red Team Tip
Operational Impacts provide real insight to the ability security operations has to defend against threats
Vulnerabilities will be discovered and leveraged; however, vulnerabilities are a byproduct of a Red Team engagement, not the focus. A Red Team's true value is assisting the target identify administrative, technical, and procedural controls that limit impacts to the organization even when vulnerable to the latest "zero-day vulnerability".

Operational Impacts

As with any security assessment, risk is what moves an organization to act. Operational impacts are a Red Team's tool to demonstrate these risks. Impacting an organization's operational capability is one of the most effective methods of showing risk to an organization's senior leadership.

Operational impacts are actions or effects performed against a target and are designed to demonstrate physical, informational, and operational weaknesses in security. Operational impacts can be thought of actions taken against an organization that impacts how it operates. These impacts can be as general as performing a denial-of-service attack or more specific, such as using hijacked ICS equipment to control a city's power grid.

Impacts are typically performed at the end of an engagement; however, it is best to plan the desired effects early. Early planning allows a Red Team to use the access and capabilities gained to best position itself for the execution of the impact, known as prepositioning. Other than obtaining and maintaining access, the Red Team should limit interaction with targets of the operational impact. This ensures all engagement impact objectives can be exercised at the appropriate time. Often, the Red Team will receive a request to cause premature impacts within the target environment. These actions need careful review and consideration before execution. If these actions do not endanger the team's ability to meet other engagement objectives, they may be executed from other attack spaces and systems not critical to engagement objectives. If actions directly conflict with engagement objectives, the Red Team Lead must ensure that the ECG and TA fully and completely understand the ramifications of each action (to include future operational impacts).

The level of depth and the impact can be as "painful " as an organization is willing to explore. These impacts are typically performed against live production systems to have the highest level of fidelity but can be executed on test and development environments if they are representative.

Focus Point

Test environments rarely model production to the level where operational impacts are felt. The technologies may match, but the people and processes typically do not. Focusing on only the test environment can lead to an unrealistic view of how the impact affects an organization.

Buy-in from management for permission to perform operational impacts can be very difficult. If an organization is highly risk-averse, these impacts may seem too costly or dangerous. Organizations that expose their systems to a full-scale attack that includes operational impacts will definitely feel the pain. However, detailed planning and execution limits real-world impacts, manages potential risks, identifies gaps in both security and operations, and provides extremely valuable lessons learned to all stakeholders.

Deconfliction

Deconfliction is the ability to identify which activity is generated by the Red Team and which is not. In general, Deconfliction:
- Separates Red Team activity from real-world activity
- Requires prior coordination through a deconfliction process
- Mandates Red Team receipt of incident-specific defensive logs
- Is not to be used as a Red Team identification process
- Requires all detected incidents, whether real-world or alleged Red Team activity, immediately be reported using normal incident reporting processes
- May require the White Cell POC to contact the Red Team's POC to determine if discovered activities are the result of the Red Team

It is critical for personnel at all levels of the engagement to be able to quickly and correctly distinguish Red Team activity from real-world attacks. Several factors can alleviate confusion and the dissemination of misinformation; however, these four simple actions go a long way in the deconfliction process:
- Ensuring Trusted Agents/White Cell understand the actions and impacts of activities as they occur
- Ensuring all Operator Logs (OPLOGS) are accurately and thoroughly completed
- Providing OPLOGS and activity lists to the ECG as requested
- Exchanging periodic Situation Reports with the White Cell

Deconfliction Process and Documentation

At a minimum, deconfliction documentation should include:

- Dates of the engagement
- POC for the engagement
    - Lead
    - Tech

- - ECG/TA/Whitecell
- Source of activities
- Destination of activities (as appropriate for the engagement type)
  - Segment, Range, Application, Host, IP, Building, Campus, etc.
  - In most scenarios, the destination is not provided
    - Deconfliction performed via TA/Whitecell
- Description of the activity

In the event deconfliction is requested, the Red Team Lead should work with the responsible TA/White Cell POC, assess the information, and isolate the information from Red Team activity. This process may include:
- Halting all activities in the area of the incident
- Reviewing the ROE for limitations, objectives, and deconfliction instructions
- Reviewing OPLOGS to determine the activities the team was conducting at the time indicated
- Confirming or denying Red Team activities for each deconfliction incident
- Confirming findings with the ECG, White Cell, and TA
- Ensuring findings are relayed by email as well as by telephone
- Maintaining records of deconfliction information, actions, assessment, and findings

If the deconfliction process indicates the Red Team is the originator:
- Determine and isolate the specific activities and scripts employed (if required)
- Determine and isolate the specific logs supporting the time frame of the incident
- Notify the Engagement Control Group

The deconfliction process provides an avenue for an engagement to be "gamed" and is susceptible to biased information flows. Part of the engagement planning process should include determining the amount of time required to execute the deconfliction process and when to use it properly.

Always emphasize there is no scenario where deconfliction will be used by the target environment or defenders to identify Red Team sources or activities. At no time should the target environment or defenders be provided with information outside the deconfliction process, except for safety or legal incidents.

Deconfliction Process

1. All alerts and incidents, whether real-world or alleged Red Team activity, should immediately be reported and acted upon in accordance with standard incident response policies and practices.
2. The appropriate read-in security operations, incident response, threat intelligence, or management personnel (e.g., Trusted Agent) will promptly notify the Red Team Lead (or designated proxy) of any reported incidents. This notification must include the source, destination, action, time of action, and alert source.
3. The appropriate response team will continue to perform operations per policy and practice.
4. The Red Team Lead will determine if the alert or activity was generated or performed by the Red Team. This determination will be made by a thorough event operator log review as well as direct operator interaction.
5. The Red Team Lead will provide the Trusted Agent a confirmation or denial of Red Team activity.
    a. If the activity is real, deconfliction is complete.
        i. The Read Team will stand down on any assets involved in the incident (if used) or temporarily add those assets to a restricted assets list.
        ii. The response team will continue operations
    b. If Red Team activity, deconfliction activities will continue.

i. The Trusted Agent must not provide this information to the security or response team until after completing the process
6. The Red Team Lead and the trusted agent will evaluate the following for determining what (if any) information should be provided to the response team:
   a. The extent to which the activity will cause unnecessary notification of senior organizational management
   b. Activities to be performed by the response team in accordance with policies and practices
   c. How response activities will impact the availability and effectiveness of the team to detect, identify, and respond to other incidents
   d. How response activities will impact the systems and networks of the incident location
   e. How response activities will impact daily operations for those outside the appropriate response teams
   f. Amount of effort required to accurately identify and isolate the Red Team vs. the benefits of responding to the incident for training, tooling, and metrics purposes
7. The evaluation actions can be agreed upon by the Red Team Lead and Trusted agent or, if required, escalated to the appropriate management level (ECG) for approval.
8. The Incident evaluation recommendation should indicate if Red Team and response teams will continue full-scope activities, if the information will be provided to constrain activities to an acceptable level of effort, or if operations will be halted.
   a. If no information is provided to the response team, full-scope activities should resume. The response teams should not be notified of Red Team activity.
   b. If information is provided, all teams must log the information and time provided and the response teams

should proceed with response activities using the provided information as "Threat Intelligence" or "guidelines."
   c. If specific actions are determined to be too high level of effort all teams must adjust current activity to accommodate the exclusion of effort. This can be:
      i. Continuance of Red Team but halt of response activities
      ii. Continuance of response but halt of Red Team activities
      iii. Continuance of Red Team but reduced response activities
      iv. Continuance of response but reduced Red Team activities
      v. Or halt of all activities
9. Final deconfliction determinations will be actioned and recorded for event reporting as well as after-action review

After Action Reviews may be used to stimulate improvements to the deconfliction process as well as incident response or other security operations.

Data Handling

General guidelines to handling data generated or gathered during a Red Team engagement is critical. All Red Team members should be responsible for safeguarding all target (a.k.a. customer) data, including:
- Personally, Identifiable Information (PII) — information that can be used to uniquely identify, contact, or locate a single person or that can be used with other sources to uniquely identify a single individual
- Privacy Act information in accordance with established regulations, policies, and procedures for handling restricted and sensitive information
- Other Industry BBP data

A Red Team should avoid the data mining of files containing Privacy Act, medical, justice, worship or religious pursuit, or any other protected or privileged information. If protected or privileged information is encountered, the Red Team should pause actions gaining or providing access, protect the information, notify the ECG, and return it to the target environment (or properly dispose of it as appropriate to the data type per ROE).

A Red Team is normally authorized to exploit files, email, or message traffic stored on the network or communications transiting the network for analysis specifically related to the accomplishment of the objectives (e.g., identifying user IDs, passwords, or network IP addresses in order to gain further access); however, each Red Team member should ensure all information exploited is necessary and within the scope of the engagement. A Red Team should not modify or delete any production user data or conduct any denial-of-service attacks unless specifically requested or authorized to do so by the ECG or ROE. The team should not otherwise intentionally degrade or disrupt normal operations of the targeted systems being exploited.

Red Team Operators must follow the provisions as set in the ROE. A properly documented ROE will contain guidance and rules related to permissions, authorizations, permitted actions, data collection requirements, and target space details. All Red Team members must adhere to the permissions granted during engagement planning.

Controls

The controls around handling client data should be agreed upon and documented in the ROE. These controls are critical. Remember, a Red Team is given the privilege to "play on someone else's playground." This access must be respected, and the data captured must be protected.

General controls and suggestions to consider when safeguarding sensitive data follow. Adjust them as required and incorporate them into your ROE template.

Policy Controls
Policy controls implemented by the Red Team should include:
- A Red Team Non-Disclosure Agreement signed by each Red Team member
- Data training (identifying and avoiding PII, PIA data, etc.)
- Ethics training
- Individual background checks

Physical Controls
Multiple levels of physical controls should exist to protect engagement tools and operating systems from intentional or unintentional loss. Red Team personnel should be familiar with all physical controls employed (e.g., locks, identification stickers, safes, storage cabinets, and lockable strongboxes) and their appropriate usage. Every Red Team member is personally responsible for the protection of target data.

The recommended security mechanisms for securing target assets include:
- Tools, computing systems, and target data should be stored inside an isolated, secured room and controlled only by the Red Team.
- Minimize contact between the team and external entities (physical internal/external access controls into the Red Team space/setup).
- When not in use, all data and equipment should be removed and placed into lockable cases, safes, or storage cabinets.
- When traveling, laptops and hard drives will be secured (in a hotel safe, tethered, in a tethered lockbox, etc.) at all times and never left unsecured in a car, hotel, customer space, etc.
- All visitors to a Red Team space will be escorted.
- Target data should be handled only by Red Team personnel with a need to know.

- At the conclusion of the engagement, all target information will be returned to the customer or destroyed using defined procedures.

Software Controls

The following software controls, designed to ensure the confidentiality, anonymity, and safety of information should be employed:
- Each host and guest operating system should be encrypted
- Use an effective password policy, and consider (should use) a multifactor protected password database to store unique passwords for each engagement
- Each host and guest operating system should be protected with a "strong" password
- Each host and guest operating system should employ a host-based firewall specific to the engagement
- When possible, communications should be encrypted
- Note, the Red Team should never use unsecured file systems or communications for team-developed engagement operations (i.e., FTP, Telnet, HTTP, VNC, WEP, etc.)
- Use (more) secure mechanisms for communications (i.e., HTTPS, WebDAV, SSH, radmin, RDP, etc.)
- The data and tools utilized during an engagement should be stored in an encrypted container and moved to the working directory only when needed
- All systems, storage, data, and tools should be encrypted at all times (data in transit, data at rest)
- The use of well-known and community-tested high-strength encryption algorithms is recommended
- All data and tools transferred to or from target systems should be hashed using MD5, SHA1, or SHA256 and added to the OPLOG as discussed in the Data Collection section
- All access, movement, and use of data and tools should be added to the OPLOG

- If a tool is no longer needed for a task, it should be removed from the target environment
- All Red Team tools and software should be removed from the target environment at the end of the engagement. If cleanup is not possible, the TA and ECG should be notified and provided with the appropriate details.

Two Person Integrity (TPI)
A key factor in data collection and execution is two-person integrity (TPI). Two-person integrity (used to verify activities performed during the engagement) should be maintained at all times. A team member should review, understand, and provide a "sanity check" for each action/command performed. That team member should verify the actions of the executing team member as well as verify the completion of the log entry. TPI helps protect both the Red Team and the target/customer against the potential release of sensitive information, violation of legal requirements/laws, and violation of the ROE. More often, TPI prevents the Red Team from making simple errors and mistakes in operation (this is further explored in the see tradecraft guidance, consult with peers section).

Key Chapter Takeaways

Engagement Planning is crucial to effectively managing potential engagement risks, successfully executing to achieve the desired goals and objectives, and providing the information required to improve both organizational and defensive capabilities. Although all planning elements play an important role in engagement success, be especially mindful to place additional attention on:

- Roles and Responsibilities
- Rules of Engagement
- Threat Planning
- Operational Impacts
- Deconfliction
- Data Handling
- Funding

Homework

1) Create a red team operations charter and methodology guide
2) Create a roles and responsibility document
3) Create a threat profile template
4) Develop a standard ROE template
5) Develop a deconfliction template
6) Develop a data handling guideline
7) Continue adding definitions to the red team lexicon

Engagement Execution

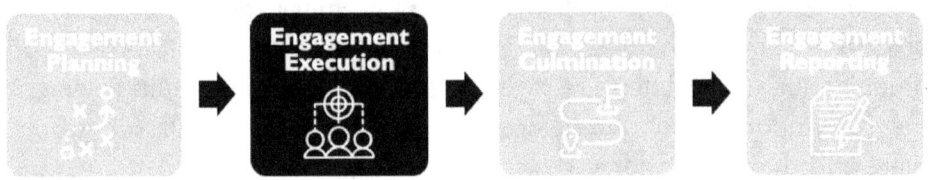

Engagement execution starts when event information and planning documentation is finalized, and preparatory actions for conducting the engagement begins. The execution phase is simply the practical application of the "why" and "how" from planning (think infrastructure buildout and engagement activities).

Data Repository

All data collected during an engagement must be logged, filed according to data type, and stored in an engagement-specific repository. This repository should be located on an encrypted volume within a centralized server / NAS /file share that is mountable or accessible only after authentication.

If at an offsite location, and a practical approach is to designate a laptop and create an authenticated directory for storing engagement data. Ensure this directory is copied to another laptop daily. Remember, the file system should be stored in accordance with policy, physical, and software controls, as previously discussed.

As operations begin, the Red Team Lead should mount the engagement-specific volume within the repository (an encrypted volume requiring authentication). Once completed, each Red Team Operator will need to mount the directory locally for engagement use (requires user authentication). At end-of-day, each operator must unmount the directory, and the Red Team Lead should unmount the repository volume.

A proven and recommended method for secure collaborative access to a common repository is mounting a remote file system over SSH. This method requires authentication for access and leverages an encrypted transport mechanism.

There are numerous ways to perform this task. A quick example is shown below:

1) Install SSHFS:
```
apt-get install sshfs
```

2) Create a "data" directory to be used for collection:
```
Mkdir /data
```

3) Mount the common repository via SSHFS by entering the password. Note: The Red Team Lead should have created an event hierarchy (as discussed in File Hierarchy) prior to this step.
```
sshfs -o allow_other,defer_permissions
redteammember1@<target>:/path_to_engagement_repository/
/data
```

4) Alternatively, mount the common repository via SSHFS using keys:
```
sshfs -o
allow_other,defer_permissions,IdentityFile=~/.ssh/id_rsa
redteammember1@<target>:/path_to_engagement_repository/
/data
```

5) Utilize:
```
ls /data
```

6) To unmount the file system:

```
unmount /data
```

More usage guidance on sshfs can be found with the sshfs man page (`man sshfs`) or at https://linux.die.net/man/1/sshfs.

While the following structure and method are not required for Red Team operations, it is HIGHLY recommended if other data collection processes or tools do not exist. Leveraging lessons learned, this structure was designed to facilitate the efficient operational flow of storing data during an engagement while improving a Red Team lead's ability to control the acquisition, flow, and reporting of information.

File Hierarchy

```
//repository/engagement_name/0-admin
```

- Administrative event information—approved IP lists, ROE, briefings, etc.

```
//repository/engagement_name/1-osint
```

- Pre-event collected OSINT information

```
//repository/engagement_name/2-recon
```

- Reconnaissance information (DNS lookups, NMAP scans, eyewitness information, etc.)

```
//repository/engagement_name/3-targets
```

- Per-target specific information (local users, file trees, command output, etc.)
- Domain-specific information (DSQUERY, domain users, domain controllers, file shares)

```
//repository/engagement_name/3-targets/ip_hostname/exfil
```

- Per-target exfiltrated data (password files, user data, diagrams, etc.). There must be a separate folder per target (ip_hostname or URL).
- File servers must each have their own EXFIL folder and be treated as separate targets for the purpose of EXFIL.

`//repository/engagement_name/4-screenshots`

- Screenshots formatted as YYYYMMDD_HHMM_IP_Description.jpg/png must be stored here no matter their source. Host-, guest-, application-, tool-, and print-screen-generated screenshots must all be copied to this location.

`//repository/engagement_name/5-payloads`

- ALL payloads (EXEs, scripts, phishing emails) must be stored under the appropriate subdirectory and entered into the OPLOG.
- This allows the team to track all payloads that are created and pushed on a target network for later cleanup, deconfliction, etc.

`//repository/engagement_name/6-logs`

- Stores all exported logs in the appropriate directory.
- The final OPLOG is stored here (example: //repository/engagement_name/6-logs/20190301_170100_OPLOGredteamconsole1.xls | csv | etc.).

`//repository/engagement_name/6-logs/redteamconsole1`

- Copy all logs to the appropriate Red system directory.
    - Raw console data (example: `//repository/engagement_name/6-`

```
logs/redteamconsole1/20190308_151312_CDT.termina
l.log.raw)
```
- Tool/application logs
  - Daily OPLOGs are stored here (example:
    ```
    //repository/engagement_name/6-
    logs/readteamconsole1/20190308_151820_OPLOG.xls|
    csv|etc.).
    ```

```
── engagement_name
    ├── 0-admin
    ├── 1-osint
    ├── 2-recon
    ├── 3-targets
    │   ├── domain_name
    │   │   └── exfil
    │   └── ip_hostname
    │       └── exfil
    ├── 4-screenshots
    │   └── YYYYMMDD_HHMM_IP_Description.png
    ├── 5-payloads
    ├── 6-logs
    └── readme.md
```

Example of the data repository file structure

Data Collection

The collection of data drives the value of the engagement itself. Data collection should be complete, enable the replication of activities and results, and identify items of significant interest to the operators. Final data sets should include:

- Pre-event data (OSINT, ROE, POC list, etc.)
- Execution data
    - **Operator** logs (manual data collection)
    - **Automated** data collection and logs
    - Screenshots
- Post-event data (data archive, closeout brief if performed, and final report)

Activity Logs

All activities related to the Red Team operation should be logged as soon as the engagement begins and only terminate after all activity related to the engagement is completed.

Examples of events to be logged include:
- Scanning activities
- Exploit events
- Stimulation efforts
- Deconfliction requests
- Target information discovered
- Targets acquired and lost
- System events (outages, downtime, etc.)
- Login attempts
- Credentials captured
- Credentials used
- Files system modifications
- Modifying or disabling security controls
- Modification or suppression of security alerts or logs
- Methods of access
- Methods of persistence employed
- Command and Control channels established
- Requests to increase, decrease, or pause activity
- ROE conflicts, requests, and modifications

All data collected during the engagement should be logged, filed according to data type, and stored in an engagement-specific file share, preferably in real time. As discussed in the Handling Client Data section, this file share should be located on a mountable, encrypted volume within a centralized server or NAS.

> **Focus Point**
>
> It's important to impose the value of failed actions. Many operators capture only successful actions performed during the engagement. In many instances, the failure of a specific action (and its associated details) provides more value to the target as well as to the Red Team than many successes.

Operator Logs

As stated previously, all activities should be logged accurately and concisely. At a minimum, the following information must be collected and logged for each action performed:
- Start Timestamp (UTC Recommended)
- End Timestamp (UTC Recommended)
- Source IP (Attack/Test System IP address)
- Source Hostname
- Destination IP (Target IP Address)
- Destination Hostname
- Destination Port (Target Port)
- Destination System Name
- Pivot IP (if applicable, list IP of any system used as a pivot, port forwarder, etc.)
- Pivot Hostname
- Pivot Ports (if applicable, list send and receive ports leveraged in pivot system)

- URL (Note, it is important to capture the FULL URL of the Target instance)
- Tool/Application
- Action (What activity or action was performed)
- Command (Full command)
- Output (Command output or response)
- Description (why or for what purpose was the action was performed)
- Result (Success, Failed, Achieved, etc.)
- System Modification (Modified file, dropped binary location, enabled functions, etc.)
- Comments
- Screenshot (File name of screenshot)
- Operator Name

Remember: When creating log entries, documenting actions, uploading/downloading files, dropping binaries, etc. It is beneficial to record using the `YYYYMMDD_HHMM_IP_Description` format.

Examples:

- Start Timestamp: Target Action
    - `20170308_151801`
- Screenshot of Nmap port 445
    - `20170308_1518_10.10.1.106_nmap445.png`
- Screenshot of open smb share
    - `20170308_1519_10.10.1.106_smb_share.png`
- Screenshot of password file
    - `20170308_1525_10.10.1.106_smb_share_passwords.txt`

Detailed logs provide a snapshot of where an operator is during an engagement and can be used to derive the status of an engagement as a whole. This type of information is critical to tracing steps throughout an engagement to properly manage, resolve deconfliction requests, and ensure data is available to produce a quality deliverable or report. Logs should contain all major steps that provide the who, what, when, where, why, and how of an action or series of actions. In addition to a text log, a screenshot is an excellent way to visualize an action. Once an engagement is complete, logs are all that remain. The quality of an engagement is directly related to the quality of the logs.

Automated Data Collection

Where available, the Red Team should leverage the use of tools and scripts to capture and consolidate engagement data.

Automated data collection alone will never be sufficient to capture the details required of a well written final report; however, it can be useful in capturing the raw data needed to validate activities, reproduce results, and support recommendations. Automated collection, if employed properly, complements the Red Team workflow and enables the operator to continue operations with the manual capture of data pertinent to the activity performed.

Terminal Logs

All Red Team engagement systems should have automated collection of raw terminal/console data. Each command should be prefixed with the operator's IP address and UTC timestamp. While there are many methods of automating this tagging and collection (TMUX, Script, Screen, etc.), it's more important that data is accurately captured than be captured in a different manner. Simply saving these tagged logs to a location such as `/root/logs/terminal/` can significantly simplify the consolidation of terminal logs.

Commercial Tools

Most commercial tools used for penetration testing or Red Teaming inherently have some level of logging capability. Some have the ability to redirect log outputs to a specific location, while others require the operator to trigger log generation. In either case, it is recommended that these logs be captured and stored in a location such as `/root/logs/commercial_tool/`.

Custom Tools

Any capable Red Team will have custom tools either generated for all events or created for a specific engagement. These tools should leverage the ability to create logs during execution. When building these tools, the Red Team should consider capturing all data required of the Operator Log and quite possibly creating log entries in the process. Each data point should be captured in the same `YYYYMMDD_HHMM_IP_Description` format (for example, `20170308_151312_UTC.terminal.log.raw`).

Consolidation

The daily transfer of these logs to the engagement repository is recommended. The preference should be to create a backup or rollup script that copies each set of logs to the repository when executed at end-of-day.

Screenshots!

Details concerning Red Team actions are often met with disbelief. Even when the team has undeniable evidence of access to a highly restrictive application, network, or physical area, target personnel (management as well as employees) sometimes have issues conceding that access was obtained. Images provide the visual proof often required.

Screenshots of activities provide validity for the actions that occurred in an assessment. Keep in mind a Red Team engagement isn't a vulnerability assessment or penetration test. The engagement is designed to "tell a story" as to how a legitimate threat could impact the function of the target environment. How better to tell that story than to include screenshots of applications, systems, and commands in the storyline?

During physical assessments, pictures or video of buildings, offices, desks, server rooms, restricted areas, etc. are generally required for proof of entry.

A second recommendation is for the physical team to generate stickers that contain the Red Team logo. Those stickers (or markers) are placed in areas of interest and placed within the frame when pictures or video is captured.

Remember: A useful filename includes the date, time, IP, and description in the format of `YYYYMMDD_HHMM_IP_Description.jpg|png` (for example, `20170308_1518_server_room_access.png`).

Tradecraft

Term tradecraft is borrowed from the intelligence community. The Merriam-Webster.com dictionary defines tradecraft as "the techniques and procedures of espionage". Tradecraft in Red Teaming has become a more general term. It is the how and why a Red Team acts. Basically, a threat's Tradecraft uses various TTPs to emulate a specific threat. To minimize confusion, Tradecraft, TTPs, and techniques will be used interchangeably. Threat portrayal requirements directly impact a Red Team's choice of TTPs. A Red Team may choose custom, highly advanced tools to support an APT (advanced persistent threat) or use simple, "script kiddie" techniques to emulate an ordinary hacker. This range forces a Red Team to be highly diverse. They must have the ability to emulate highly advanced threats and to limit themselves to a simple threat. Remember, Tradecraft and TTPs are core to a Red Team. Weak Tradecraft equals a weak Red Team. A Red Team must be highly capable in order to successfully emulate a threat with the fidelity needed to accomplish their goals as a threat.

General Guidance

Maintaining consistent TTPs is essential during Red Team engagements. Getting caught or stimulating an effect at the wrong time in the engagement can compromise an entire mission. Guidance on TTPs "do's and don'ts" for Red Team engagements are included below. These rules must always be applied to the first set of operating procedures. This ruleset is a great starting point for developing high-level TTPs.

If circumstances require a deviation, or a rule does not fit an engagement, a consultation with a senior Red Team Operator is required. Anytime a TTP rule is violated, senior staff should be involved in the decision and the reason and circumstances documented.

Log all significant actions (successes and failures)

Bottom line up front: Log, log, and log some more! Take screenshots of all significant actions, including successful and failed attempts.

One of the most important aspects of the Red Team engagement is the collection of data (a.k.a. logs). It is extremely common that an inexperienced team completes an engagement with subpar documentation. Many actions are not fully captured, some actions are never captured, and often key failures are ignored. Each action performed provides value to the target as well as the target defenders. Incomplete logs prevent the Red Team from providing a complete and accurate depiction of the actions, obstacles, and defensive strengths and weaknesses of the target (a.k.a. Red Team mission failure).

As previously covered, there are several methods to ensure that logs are appropriately captured and stored:
- Automated logging of the terminal: All terminal actions are logged, timestamped, and saved to a predefined location
- Tool logs: Most commercial tools have some capability to log actions and produce a raw or a final report
- Custom tools logs: If you write a custom tool/script, it should output a log of actions and results
- Operator logs: By far, these are the most important logs. A log may show the action performed and the result; however, only the

operator can accurately note the way the action was performed, which led them to the decision, and their interpretation of the result
- Screenshots: Terminal logs are great for the operator and even better as supporting artifacts; however, they may mean nothing to senior-level executives (or even to some IT professionals). Screenshots before, during, and following the execution of an action hold much more weight than a terminal log, tool log, or operator log (often, it may just be a screenshot of the terminal during execution)

Consult with Peers

No matter how long you have been performing IT or security, consult your peers before taking action. This is especially true during exploitation and Command and Control setup. Simple mistakes often lead to Red Team discovery too early in the engagement. Look at the command below. The command could be run as to provide general situational awareness on a Linux system. What is the expected output of the following command?
`netstat -antb`

The command above is a netstat command that can be executed on a Windows host. Linux does not have the "b" option and produces an "`invalid option`" response. Think about it:

Have you ever typed `ifconfig` instead of `ipconfig`?

Have you ever typed `rm *` in the wrong directory?

Have you ever entered credentials only to discover they were "fat fingered" (after an access error)?

While these are oversimplifications, they represent the need for peer review on tools, C2, setup, execution, and even cleanup. Mistakes can lead to accidental exposure on a Red Team engagement. This can cause significant setbacks and reduce the quality of an engagement.

Understand the Tools and Technologies Used

Knowing what functionality a tool provides is only one-third of the equation. Before a new tool (script, application, binary, process, etc.) is used on a target system, it must be tested, undergo an internal vetting process and be added to an official toolset.

So how do we complete the equation? By asking:
- What artifacts does the tool leave behind?
- Are any files modified during execution?
- Are there tales in the network traffic?
- Does the tool have negative impacts on specific versions of an OS? (It works fine on Windows 8 but causes a system error on Windows 10)
- Does the tool attempt to run as a specific user or, worse, create a user/group?
- Does the tool try to call home for updates?
    - This can trigger defensive alerts identifying unauthorized persons or software on the network

Think about psexec.. What is it? The most common answer refers to the PsExec.exe tool from SysInternals[13].

What does it do? At a high level, it executes commands on local or remote Windows system.

What does it do in terms of indicators?
- Copies a service file to the remote system
- Enters a service key into the Registry
- Creates a prefetch file
- Creates an entry in the Application Compatibility Cache
- Creates a login event

---

[13] "PsExec - Windows Sysinternals | Microsoft Docs." 28 Jun. 2016, https://docs.microsoft.com/en-us/sysinternals/downloads/psexec

- Creates a profile folder for the remote user
- Attempts to remove the service file and key when exiting (not always successful)

What happens when using the –e option? –s option?
How does this differ from psexec for PowerShell?

In short, you must understand how tools or technique interacts with a target, what network traffic it may generate, and what traces it may leave behind. In the case of psexec, this can be considered a lateral movement technique instead of a specific tool. There are multiple methods of achieving the result PsExec.exe provide without the tool itself.

Perform Situational Awareness

After gaining access to a remote system or application, perform situational awareness before moving on.
- Understand the environment you are in. (Is the target in scope?)
- What protections exist on the system or network?
- What are the risks of being caught, and what attack paths does the system provide?
- Are there pre-established connections to other network resources?
- Who is currently logged into the system?
- Who has recently logged into the system?

Minimize callback (C2) volume

Unless a host-based protection mechanism is triggered, it is more likely to be discovered or caught by a defender's recognition or analysis of traffic on the network. To avoid early detection follow good tradecraft procedure to limit and control the amount of traffic generated during an engagement. There are several general concepts that, if followed, increase the success of the engagement while decreasing the chances of being discovered:

- Keep traffic internal to a network: One of the most common issues, and one you should always attempt to change, is the limited number of sensors inside a network. Most network protections are currently applied at the boundary.
- Pivot Command and Control traffic to a minimal number of outbound sources: Maintain at least two outbound sources for C2 redundancy; however, use only one for operations (considered an interactive tier). The second (a long- or short-haul tier) is dormant or extremely slow and used as a backup if/when the primary is discovered.

Do not use unencrypted channels for C2 (unless blending into network traffic)

Command and Control data exiting the network must be encrypted. An IDS or other network defense will detect cleartext data, such as uploading a binary, issuing an operating system command, or using a web shell. It has become common for IPSs/IDSs to detect specific strings discovered in cleartext traffic. For example, "C:\Windows\System32" has become a common trigger for investigation.

Some defenders have even gone the extra mile in legitimizing a potential threat. Assume the defenders or IT staff uses a remote administration tool regularly. Ignoring recommendations, this traffic is unencrypted. Rather than causing an alert each time the tool is used legitimately; the alert is configured to look for inconsistencies in the usage. For example, most attackers are accustomed to typing lowercase commands in Windows. The defender ignores "C:\Windows\System32" but alerts on "c:\windows\system32"

Internal encryption is another example of where peers should be consulted to determine the best course of action before deploying C2 further into a network.

The encryption of internal C2 traffic depends upon several different factors:
- Are there sensors inside the network?
- Are there other encrypted communications occurring between target systems?
- Would encrypted traffic stand out more than unencrypted traffic?

Do not attempt to exploit or attack unencrypted websites or applications

As tempting as it may be, do not attack unencrypted websites. Simple attacks can trigger IDSs. Always know your target IP space. There are likely several websites available for review. Proper reconnaissance or coordination should have discovered each. Create a list of sites in your target log. Include IP addresses, URLs, an educated guess at the functions, ports, protocols, etc.

Focus Point

Prior to performing any exploitation and attacks against a web server, refer to your Rules of Engagement and fully understand:
- Who actually owns the website?
- Who owns the system where the website is hosted?
- Who owns the back-end application?
- Have proper approvals been obtained for testing?

Do not execute from non-executable locations

- Execution in a Windows environment must occur in a location typical of Windows
- Executable locations such as c:\programdata, c:\progam files, and c:\windows\ are common

- Execution from locations such as c:\windows\temp should never occur or be used with an understanding of risk

Do not use binaries for initial capabilities

As a general rule, do not drop binaries on the system. First, use built-in commands to achieve your goals. This is not always possible, and binaries may be required; however, binaries **must** be vetted, obfuscated, and tested against detection before use.
- Ensure all other "Do's and Don'ts" are met for all binaries
- Consult a senior operator before dropping any binary

Do not download restricted datasets

NEVER download (or remove from the target network) any PII, HIPAA, PCI, or other restricted datasets. A good rule of thumb is to annotate the type of data, location, access method, and level of access to restricted data in the log.
- Ensure the log notes include a reference to the type of data discovered for quick reference
- Take a screenshot of the displayed filename and location (assuming the filename has no restricted data included)
- Screenshot a portion of the dataset without capturing the restricted data. The operator may do so for proof of access.
- If the data set is of concern, attempt to copy the file to a new name in the same location. This will validate access without exposing the data.
- DO NOT take screenshots of the data itself!

Execution Concepts

Exploits

Exploitation is a technique a threat uses to take advantage of a vulnerability or weakness. This can be due to a software flaw or misconfiguration. Unlike penetration testing, where validating exploits against a vulnerability is a primary goal, exploitation is not an end goal for Red Team engagements. Exploits are merely a means to an end; however, this does not reduce their importance. Exploitation can be a critical part of a Red Team engagement. Exploitation must be used with caution as many often trigger a Blue response. As with all decisions made during a Red Team engagement, risk vs. reward must be measured to determine if the access gained from an exploit is worth the potential exposure.

Exploits should be used to gain access only as a means to an end. Once exploitation occurs, backdoors or other means of access should be established. The exploit should not be used as a means to regain access to a target. For instance, assume a known remote code execution flaw exists in a web application. A readily available public exploit exists, and using such an exploit may trigger a security device, like an IDS. A Red Team weighs the risk and decides to move forward with the exploit. A Red Team operator successfully uses the exploit from a burnable IP space. The exploit results in remote command execution of the target webserver. Instead of using the exploit repeatedly to issue commands, a web shell is deployed. This web shell can now be accessed from a different source address. In this way, the exploit is used only one time. The web shell provides a useable backdoor to access the webserver for further actions.

Exploiting Known Vulnerabilities

A threat will use what is available. Like real attackers, Red Teams will take advantage of a weakness to support their goals. There is a key difference in how a Red Team should view and use an exploit vs. other types of security testing. In Red Teaming, known (including pre-packaged or "canned") exploits should only be used to directly support a goal. This means an environment may have multiple exploitable vulnerabilities that a Red Team does not exploit. This could be due to minimizing detection or the fact that exploitation does not support a Red Team goal. It is important to remember that a Red Team engagement is not a comprehensive view of a target's vulnerabilities.

In summary, many exploits have known signatures and can be easily detected or have code that causes unintended damage or impacts to a target. A Red Team Operator should always understand the exploit, its code, and know its IOCs to manage the risk of exposure or damage to a target.

Popular places to find exploits:
- Metasploit: www.metasploit.com – public exploits and zero days
- ExploitHub: www.exploithub.com – commercial exploit clearinghouse for nonzero days
- Exploit DB: www.exploit-db.com – repository of exploits maintained by Offensive Security
- Other exploit clearing houses

Focus Point

A target environment may have multiple exploitable vulnerabilities. Only those that enable meeting the goals and objectives of the engagement should be considered for exploitation. Document all identified exploitable vulnerabilities but use only those required to achieve engagement objectives.

Always consider the risk in every action taken.

Exploitation without Exploits

Exploitation does not always require exploit based on code flaws. Experienced penetration testers and Red Teamers will use the concept of *Exploitation without Exploits*. This is the idea of exploiting or compromising a system by using the system design, functions, and configuration against itself. Poor security controls and misconfigurations will often lead to compromise. Not only can using a system against itself support a compromise, it usually involves a smaller IOC footprint. In many cases, attacking a system without exploits looks very similar to the same activity performed by a network administrator.

There are several techniques a threat can use to exploit, compromise, or gain access to a target system. Do not fall into the trap of canned exploits being needed to achieve goals. Exploits can be rare, costly, and ephemeral. When they work, they are great, but most exploits have a short lifetime. Good Red Team Operators regularly explore and practice many means of remote exploitation or compromise. This is an ever-changing area of security. Research and practice are needed to keep current on modern techniques.

Web Application Vulnerability
Security has increased over the years, and the number of traditional memory corruption exploits has dropped significantly. This has driven threats to search for alternate means of gaining access to a target. Web applications are excellent targets for exploitation and remote code execution. Although web applications have been around for years, their security is still quite weak and misunderstood. This makes web applications prime doorways into a network as even the most basic application can provide a backdoor to a threat. In short, web applications are one of the most effective ways to gain remote access to an environment.

Security Misconfigurations

Security has improved over the years, and the number of traditional memory corruption exploits has dropped significantly. This has driven threats to search for alternate means of gaining access to a target. Web applications are excellent targets for exploitation and remote code execution. Although web applications have been around for years, their security defenses are still quite weak and misunderstood. This misunderstanding makes web applications prime doorways into a network as even the most basic application can provide a backdoor to a threat. In short, web applications can be one of the most effective ways to gain remote access to an environment.

Misconfigured network security rules often provide multiple paths for threat traversal. When systems can communicate freely in a network, they can quickly exchange information. This includes a threat's traffic. It is prevalent for an organization to configure externally facing traffic rules and leave internal network communications wide open. It is also common for credentials to be stored in cleartext in publicly available locations on a network. These credentials may be user or administrative. Either way, when threats use valid credentials, they look and feel like insiders. It can be very difficult for a Blue Team to distinguish between a threat and a valid user. These are important measurements of security operations capability.

Poor or Lack of Security Monitoring
A lack of security monitoring allows a threat to use a more extensive toolset. Tools or techniques that may be loud or trigger a response may work just fine in an unmonitored environment. This oversight provides a threat with much greater flexibility and capability. A Red Team can take advantage of an unmonitored network. A common operational impact is data exfiltration. Perhaps a target organization has propriety sensitive intellectual property. Exposures of this information could significantly harm the organization. A Red Team can test the ability a threat has to gain access and exfiltrate the data. A lack of monitoring may allow the threat to access and steal the data without being noticed. Blue Teams that have a

weak security monitoring process will not identify malicious traffic or changes made by a threat. Defensive tools are great but must be configured and tested to ensure they are operating as expected. Remember, the primary role of the Red Team is to facilitate the improvement of an organization's defensive posture.

Social Engineering (SE)
Social engineering is exploiting weaknesses in human nature. Red Team engagements often rely on social engineering to support goals. This is typically used in the following areas:

Phishing
- Sending an email to entice an end-user to provide sensitive information or to deliver a payload
- Can be used to deliver a malicious payload
- Can be used to facilitate in-person SE
- Can be used to facilitate physical access

Telephoning/Texting
- Calling or texting to entice an end-user to provide sensitive information
- Can be used to facilitate either phishing or in-person SE
- Can be used to facilitate physical access

In-person pretexting
- In-person social engineering is typically used to support a physical breach

Use Caution
Social engineering (especially Phishing) works, period. But, this is not always the best option. There are political risks associated with SE a user. For example, Phishing campaigns that work well may harass or even embarrass end users. Use caution when creating a phishing campaign. Many targets of phishing require the campaign to be approved before the emails are sent. This may protect the organization but can also limit the success rate of a phish. In cases where phishing is risky, consider white carding. A solid strategy is to send a phishing email to a trusted insider.

That person will click links or provide information as directed by the phish. This allows a phishing payload to be delivered in a politically safe manner while allowing the phishing email to touch all the security defenses. This model uses the assumption that a user will succumb to a phishing attack. The challenge for the Red Team is to bypass the security protections designed to protect users from themselves.

A phish that leads to the compromise of a single system may be acceptable. A phish that leads to the compromise of an organization is not acceptable as multiple failures must have occurred in organizational controls (technical, policy, procedural, etc.). The authors are aware these are controversial statements and provide the following concepts for thought.

Consider This

A phishing attack leading to organizational compromise is NOT the fault of an end-user. Instead, it is the insufficient security controls of a target environment!

As noted above, Social Engineering simply works. Users are often provided many different types of training on social engineering, phishing, information security, operational security, etc.; however, a well researched, constructed, and targeted phish will be successful in most scenarios. This idea has been proven multiple times by multiple professionals with multiple write-ups on techniques and successes. A well-planned phish avoids common indicators of phishing, does not alert the user to malicious intent, and can ultimately provide threat access to the end user's system. Combined with a threat's effective use of good tradecraft, the user has no "indicators of bad". At this point, the user's responsibility ends. Anything beyond (and arguably including) the initial compromise of the end user's system is the responsibility of the organization. For all intents and purposes, the threat has become a logical insider. If the threat has the capability to move laterally throughout the network, elevate privileges, access sensitive information, exfiltrate data, or cause operational impact; so do other (perhaps all) users within the organization. It's likely they just don't know how.

Tools and Tool Examples

A Red Team can and should use any tool that supports its end goals. Although many Red Teams use the same tools used by penetration testers, this does not mean tools are employed the same or chosen carelessly. A team must understand the capabilities and limits of a tool. The team must have the ability to control or tune a tool to fit the needs of an engagement; not only in technical capability but also the ability to tune a tool to model a specific threat. The choice of tools may lead to custom development, the purchase of commercial tools, or the simple use of built-in operating system commands. In the end, the toolset is chosen based on a Red Team's goals.

The way a Red Team uses common security tools can be quite different from the way of other security testers. A Red Team often needs to customize the code to ensure it performs in a specific way or change the indicators a tool may leave behind. At a minimum, a good operator must understand how a tool functions and what impact or risk is introduced to an engagement. Good Red Team operators maintain control over their actions. This includes how, when, and if a tool is used.

This section refers to many common tools used in the security community. Many of these tools are older or not appropriate for modern Red Teaming engagements. The purpose of discussion is to provide context in Red Teaming.

Vulnerability Scanners

Red Teams do not commonly use vulnerability scanners. These tools generally tend to be loud and to generate a tremendous amount of traffic.

Vulnerability identification by a Red Team focuses on OSINT, low and slow enumeration, intelligent guessing, or other non-intrusive methods. There are cases where vulnerability scanners are useful. For example, a Red Team has identified a web application built on Joomla with paths to a Red Team's goals. They would like to know if the version of Joomla is vulnerable. A standard vulnerability scanner could be employed, but this could be overkill for a single application. Instead, the team may tune a vulnerability scanner to check for a small set of Joomla-based flaws. Using a focused scan would minimize exposure. They could also manually extract version information from the web application. In any case, caution should be taken before running a vulnerability scanner to reduce exposure. If more intrusive scanning is needed, performing the scan from a burnable source that is dedicated to louder activities would protect more sensitive sources from being exposed.

In the end, the choice of when or how to use a vulnerability scanner comes to risk. Think about the following before running a vulnerability scanner:
- Does the risk of exposure from running a generally loud tool outweigh the potential knowledge learned?
- Are there other ways to identify a vulnerability without using the automated scanner?
- Will exploitation of a vulnerability provide a path that is beneficial to a Red Team's goal? (Remember that vulnerability identification is typically not a Red Team engagement goal.)

Remember This

Just because a target is vulnerable, doesn't mean it must be exploited!

NMAP and network scanning

Nmap[14] is a core tool for penetration testers and security analysts. It was written and is maintained by Fyodor[15]. Nmap is often used as a port scanner to determine the status of TCP and UDP ports on a target system. The tool is not just a simple port scanner but a highly capable network enumeration tool allowing for a large variety of enumeration techniques. It can be extended through the use of NSE (Nmap Scripting Engine) scripts. According to the Nmap documentation, the Nmap Scripting Engine (NSE) is one of Nmap's most powerful features. It allows users to write (and share) simple scripts to automate a wide variety of networking tasks. NSE scripts are extremely useful. They can be used to enumerate a system for information or to identify vulnerabilities.

In short, Nmap can be used for simple enumeration or in-depth vulnerability scanning. Its flexibility and power allow for a great deal of flexibility and capability to enumerate a target; however, this power can be a double-edged sword. Nmap is not necessarily designed to be stealthy but to be very capable. A Red Team operator must understand what indicators are being generated when using Nmap's various capabilities. This text will not go into great depth on the Nmap tool but will cover some basic usage to highlight an everyday use case for a Red Team. These concepts apply to several tools. Nmap is discussed because of its popularity and use security testing in general.

Let's look at an Nmap command with several options

```
Nmap -sT -T2 -n -Pn -oA <date/time_target> -p
80,443,8080 10.10.10.1-100
```

Here is the breakdown of the command arguments:

---

[14] "Nmap: the Network Mapper - Free Security ...." https://nmap.org/
[15] "Nmap Network Scanning—The Official Nmap Project Guide to ...." https://nmap.org/book/.

-sT
- This forces Nmap to perform a full connect scan. Nmap's default is –sS, or a stealth scan. A full scan completes the full TCP handshake (SYN,SYN/ACK,ACK) and sends a (RST) to gracefully tear down the connection. A –sS scan sends only SYN and waits for a response or timeout. A full connection is not established. Although the term stealth is used, this behavior can indicate a scan is being run against a target. In general, full connect scans produce less triggers through network security devices. This is especially true when they are executed very slowly.

-T2
- This is an Nmap timing template. They range from 0–5. The template names are paranoid (0), sneaky (1), polite (2), normal (3), aggressive (4), and insane (5).
- According to the Nmap documents, "While -T0 and -T1 may be useful for avoiding IDS alerts, they will take an extraordinarily long time to scan thousands of machines or ports. For such a long scan, you may prefer to set the exact timing values you need rather than rely on the canned -T0 and -T1 values."
- The bottomline: control the speed of a scan to balance the gathering of information with sending packets too quickly.
- Nmap has many other timing control options. Refer to the help document for details.

-Pn
- Treat all hosts as online—skip host discovery.
- This disables the default tests Nmap uses to discover if a host is online.
- If no host discovery options are given, Nmap sends an ICMP echo request, a TCP SYN packet to port 443, a TCP ACK packet to port 80, and an ICMP timestamp request. (For IPv6, the ICMP timestamp request is omitted, because it is not part of ICMPv6.) These defaults are equivalent to the -PE -PS443 -PA80 -PP options.

`-n`
- For machines on a local Ethernet network, ARP scanning will still be performed (unless --disable-arp-ping or --send-ip is specified), because Nmap needs MAC addresses to further scan target hosts. In previous versions of Nmap, -Pn was -P0 and -PN.
- Never do DNS resolution.
- This is recommended as a default. If the DNS servers are public, this is not as much of an issue. If you are using a target's DNS servers, sending DNS queries to perform a port scan may be considered unnecessary.

`-oA`
- Output in three formats (normal, greppable, and xml).
- Data collection is extremely important during a Red Team engagement. Using Nmap's built-in feature allows results to be captured and potentially parsed by other tools.

`-p`
- The ports to scan.
- Setting the specific ports is a best practice. Using Nmap's default may be helpful in finding unknown services, but a target intellectual guess can help find specific services.
- If you are looking for web servers, choose ports that would most likely be associated with your target. OSINT and recon prior to a scan will help determine the appropriate ports to enumerate.

Please note that even with these suggestions, there are situations when stealth or risk tolerance less important. Perhaps you are using Nmap to trigger a Blue response. A loud scan may be needed to gain information for access to a target. In any case, a Red Team must control their IOCs and manage their risk of exposure to meet the goals of an engagement. Understanding and controlling Red Team tools is the key takeaway for this section. This example is only a small look at Nmap. Nmap offers numerous methods of controlling its traffic. Refer to the documentation at https://nmap.org/docs.html for details.

Metasploit

The Metasploit Framework[16] is a free, open-source exploitation framework created initially by HD Moore in 2003. This tool has become a core asset to security testers of all types due to its tremendous flexibility and capability. Metasploit includes several collections of exploits, payloads, auxiliary modules, and post-exploitation modules. Metasploit is a great exploitation framework. The exploit, enumeration, and post-exploitation capabilities can provide a team with a great deal of capabilities. While Metasploit is a great resource, caution must be taken when using Metasploit's Meterpreter payload. Meterpreter is not a bad payload choice for Command and Control, but like any tool, it must be understood and adequately tuned before use. This tool has been examined and analyzed in great depths. This has led to a highly capable toolset, but it can be profiled and identified by a competent security team.

Pros and Cons of Meterpreter
PROS
- Tremendous amount of capability and flexibility
- Large contributor base
- Large selection of post-exploitation modules
- Easy to use
- Stable

CONS
- Synchronous communication.
- Well-Known IOCs. (Source code modification is required to minimize these.)

Msfconsole can be tuned using resource files. Resource files are simply a set of msfconsole commands saved to a script. If scripts are saved to: ~/.msf4/msfconsole.rc

---

[16] "Metasploit | Penetration Testing Software, Pen Testing ...." https://www.metasploit.com/.

A few recommended base msfconsole settings to consider:

```
# ~/.msf4/msfconsole.rc
spool /root/.msf4/spool.log
setg ConsoleLogging true
setg verbose true
setg LogLevel 5
setg SessionLogging true
setg TimestampOutput true
setg PromptTimeFormat %Y%m%d.%H%M%S%z
setg PROMPT %T S:%S J:%J
setg ExitOnSession false
setg DisableCourtesyShell true
load sounds #optional
```

These settings will set up console logging, increase the log verbosity, enable session logging, standardize the timestamp, add information to the console prompt, set exitonsession to keep listeners from dying, disable the courtesy shell, and load sounds. Sounds are optional but can be useful indicators when the console is not being monitored in real time. This is a small set of Metasploit msfconsole configuration settings. There are times where Metasploit source code will need to be modified to control the attack flow or manage IOCs.

In terms of where the metasploit framework fits in Red Teaming, it is useful in providing a library of exploits, but is generally not appropriate for command and control.

Web Shells

A web shell is server-side code that acts as a "shell," remote administration tool, or control panel allowing a user to issue remote commands to be executed by a web server. Whoever controls the web shell has the ability to execute operating system commands on the target web server. The successful exploitation of a web application is needed to deploy a web shell. Web shells can be written in any web language, such as PHP, ASP, ASPX, Perl, Ruby, Python, JSP, Java, etc.

Web Shell Examples
- China Chopper – A small web shell packed with features. It has several Command and Control features, including a password brute force capability
- WSO – Stands for "web shell by orb" and has the ability to masquerade as an error page containing a hidden login form
- C99 – A version of the WSO shell with additional functionality. It can display the server's security measures and contains a self-delete function
- B374K – A PHP-based web shell with common functionalities such as viewing processes and executing commands

Why would a threat use a web shell? Remote code execution flaws are limited and have forced the heavy use of client exploitation; however, web applications are still very valuable doors into a network, and directly compromising a network via remote means provides many options to a threat. Web applications are commonly overlooked, misconfigured, and riddled with flaws. Executing operating system commands with an on-demand tool is a perfect Long Haul solution and, therefore, a perfect target for a Red Team.

A Red Team must be aware of common IOCs generated by the deployment of a web shell:

- The exploitation of a web application flaw must occur
    - The server attack surface is limited to file upload flaws, RFI flaws, or application security flaws
    - This can trigger an alert depending on the type of exploitation or flaw
- Web server files will be added or modified
    - Source code modification or the direct modification of an application's source code will occur
    - Integrity monitoring may alert defenses to these changes

Although the vulnerabilities required for web shell deployment comprise a small subset of application security, those paths are worth pursuing as a threat.

Web shells are great tools but do have limits. Operating system commands executed on the target server are in the context of the web service user. If a target has followed best security practices, the service will be running as non-privileged. This may seriously limit a web shell's capability. An operator may need additional credentials or further exploitation to issue commands with the proper permissions. Even in the case of limited use, web shells can often still be used as pivot points. Other limitations depend on the web server's communication with other target systems. Web shells may have limited access to internal servers. Web servers in a DMZ or external location may require pivoting through multiple servers to communicate with internal target systems. In any engagement, the maintenance of a solid toolset that includes web shells allows a Red Team to be flexible, which increases its capability.

Command and Control (C2)

Command and Control (C2) is a cornerstone to a Red Team's ability to control and maintain control of a target. C2 is the influence an attacker has over a compromised computer system. This influence is expressed using a C2 infrastructure that can issue various tasks and instructions to the remote system.

Tools such as PowerShell Empire or Cobalt Strike provide agents or beacons that can be deployed to a target. These tools use an asynchronous means of communication. An agent or beacon polls a C2 server for instructions on a controlled interval. The server is queried for a task. If a task exists, the agent or beacon performs the action and reports the results. If there are no tasks, the agent or beacon goes to "sleep" for the predefined period of time.

C2 fall into three categories.

- Synchronous
- Asynchronous
- On-demand

Synchronous C2 operates in real-time. A constant stream of communications is required to maintain the C2 channel. Asynchronous C2 communications offer many benefits to a Red Team over synchronous communications by:
- Controlling when and how often communications are sent - A C2 agent can poll as quickly as near real-time or may check in once a day, week, or month
- Bypassing firewalls through egress communication - Clients are typically not accessible from outside a network but can reach assets on the internet through outbound communication
- Not requiring a constant, established connection

On-demand C2 is unique and operates only when needed. Communications occur only when triggered by an operator. Tools such as email or web shells can provide excellent on-demand C2 channels. Choosing your Command and Control (C2) mechanisms is a critical step in designing your C2 plan for an engagement.

C2 Channels

There are numerous methods for establishing C2. Each of these methods use a C2 Channel for primary communications. While any channel can be used, it is recommended to use a channel that blends in with organizational traffic. Commonly used C2 channels include:
- HTTP/HTTPS
- DNS
- SMB

- SSH

HTTP/HTTPS - Hyper text Transfer Protocol
- Communicate over common web protocols
- Associated TCP ports 80/443 usually allowed to egress
- Blend in with typical network traffic
- SSL adds an additional layer of protection of the traffic's true intent

DNS – Domain Name System
- Communicate via the internet's DNS infrastructure
- Avoid direct connections between compromised host and C2 server
- Bypass the most stringent network egress restrictions
- Can appear anomalous if DNS logging is enabled and monitored

SMB - Server Message Block
- Utilize SMB to communicate via named pipes
- Ideal for internal network lateral movement in Windows environments

VPN/SSH/CITRIX – Remote Access Tools
- Utilize existing legitimate remote access tools hosted on the network

Establishing a C2 Infrastructure

A well thought out and designed C2 plan can make the difference between a successful or a failed engagement. The C2 environment is the heart and lifeline for all threat communications.

As part of creating and maintaining an infrastructure for your Red Team operations, you will need the following at a minimum:

- A variety of domain names—preferably .com, .net, and .org sites related to the organization(s) being assessed
    - Ensure domains are properly categorized (BlueCoat, WebPulse, OpenDNS, PhishTank)
    - Use Top Level Domains (TLD) common to your target area or usage
- Valid SSL certificates for those domains

- Internet-accessible servers (VPS or physical)
    - Separated for phishing, redirecting, and C2 servers
- Installed and configured C2 platforms

For more information, detailed C2 design information is maintained regularly by Jeff Dimmock (@bluescreenofjeff[17]) can be found at the following:
- Designing Effective Covert Red Team Attack Infrastructure – https://bluescreenofjeff.com/2017-12-05-designing-effective-covert-red-team-attack-infrastructure/#references
- Red Team Infrastructure Wiki – https://github.com/bluscreenofjeff/Red-Team-Infrastructure-Wiki

C2 Tools

Although Red Teams use similar offensive security tools as that of penetration testers, there are tools more emphasized by Red Teams—specifically, when it comes to Command and control. While other security testers may use Command and Control tools, as well, a Red Team's goals are typically heavily dependent on a solid C2 infrastructure and toolset.

Some of the most popular C2 toolsets have been Cobalt Strike, PowerShell Empire, and Metasploit. All the tools share a heavy emphasis on supporting post-exploitation. Although the tools may have an exploitation capability, a Red Team's focus is on their use for post-exploitation and use of C2 for the duration needed.

---

[17] "Jeff Dimmock (@bluscreenofjeff) | Twitter." https://twitter.com/bluscreenofjeff.

> **2019, Year of the C2**
>
> In and around the year 2019, tremendous growth in the number of C2 frameworks occurred. Dozens of C2 frameworks were released or seriously updated. This increase provided new options to Red Teams by providing new protocols, more cross-platform support, and new operator interfaces.

CobaltStrike[18]

- Commercial software from Strategic Cyber, LLC.
- Command and Control payload is known as a beacon
- An earlier project, Armitage, is a free tool by Raphael Mudge. It is often confused with the free version of Cobalt Strike but has a very different code base
- Described as "Cobalt Strike is software for Adversary Simulations and Red Team Operations."
- Supports both asynchronous and synchronous C2 communication

Empire[19]

- Open source software
- Command and Control payload is known as an agent
- Described as "Empire is a pure PowerShell post-exploitation agent built on cryptologically-secure communications and a flexible architecture."
- Supports both asynchronous and synchronous C2 communication
- Officially retired as a project in 2019

---

[18] "Cobalt Strike." https://www.cobaltstrike.com/..
[19] "PowerShell Empire | Building an Empire with PowerShell." https://www.powershellempire.com/.

Tweet announcing the retirement of Empire

Metasploit

- Open source and commercial software is maintained by Rapid7
- Highly capable penetration testing and exploitation framework with some Red Team post-exploitation support
- Command and Control payload is known as Meterpreter
- Communication is generally synchronous

Other C2

Cobalt Strike, Empire, and Metasploit are simply three C2 examples selected due to being commonly known and widely used. In 2018 and 2019 numerous tools and frameworks for command and control were announced and released. This trend will likely continue for future years. If building a C2 framework isn't possible given the team's time or budget, the authors recommend a simple search for potential frameworks, testing of each, and selecting the framework(s) that best meet the need for the current effort.

C2 Redirectors

C2 redirectors are pivots designed to separate communications between a target and C2 servers. They are designed to protect the C2 servers' IP addresses from identification. Redirectors are what the target will see as malicious. The target may observe any IP address or domain name associated with a redirector. If a defender identifies malicious activity, they may block a redirector IP address. Redirectors should be treated as burnable. If burned, a Red Team Operator can simply switch to an alternate redirector for pivoting C2 traffic from the target to the C2 server.

Redirectors and C2 servers must be protected. Command and Control servers must communicate with the target over the C2 channel, such as HTTPS on port 443. Efforts to limit (or drop) C2 connections from unexpected networks should be made; however, this is not the only communication to a C2 server. An operator must use the C2 interface to control the server and issue commands. This must also be protected. ACLs or other protections should be put in place only to allow access from Red Team Operators. A responsible Red Team should not allow C2 control outside designated Red Team IPs/Segments. Even "hacker" software is not safe.

Given that thought, proper security and access controls effectively limit the risk of new vulnerabilities or unknown access methods in Red Team tools. For example, in September 2016, a remote code execution flaw was found in Cobalt Strike 3.5. This flaw allowed remote code execution on the C2 server via a malicious beacon. Effective access controls, if employed, significantly limit the likelihood of compromise from any network other than Red Team, redirector, or target.

Virtual Private Services such as Amazon EC2, Digital Ocean, and Linode are great solutions to create internet-accessible redirectors. Redirector servers can be easily deployed or torn down. Most service providers offer an API that allows the deployment and destruction of redirectors to be scripted and automated. Redirectors can be made to be highly resistant to removal or to be even more obfuscated. Techniques such as Domain Fronting[20] take advantage of the trust in highly trusted CDNs. A reverse HTTP proxy, such as Apache mod_rewrite, can be used to tune HTTP traffic to obfuscate better or hide malicious traffic.

Deploying Redirectors

There are several ways to redirect traffic. Here are a couple of quick examples for Linux and Windows 'dumb pipe' redirectors. A dumb pipe redirctors is the process of redircting traffic from on TCP port to another.

---

[20] "Domain Fronting - Enterprise | MITRE ATT&CK™." 16 Jan. 2018, https://attack.mitre.org/techniques/T1172/.

Linux:

Create a cron job to start a socat script that redirects TCP 443 from the redirector to 10.10.10.10:

```
crontab -e
@reboot /usr/bin/socat TCP-LISTEN:443,fork /
TCP:10.10.10.10:443 &
```

Windows:

Use the netsh command to create a persistent port redirection rule that redirects TCP 443 from the redirector to 10.10.10.10:

```
netsh interface portproxy add v4tov4 listenport=443
listenaddress=10.20.20.20 connectport=443
connectaddress=10.10.10.10
```

There are several methods and techniques for redirection. The examples in this book focus on exposing the need that redirectors are critical to an engagement. Red Team operators must include a set of processes and technical approaches in the Red Team toolbox.

C2 Tiers

Designing a robust C2 infrastructure involves creating multiple layers of Command and Control. These can be described as tiers. Each tier offers a level of capability and covertness. The idea of using multiple tiers is the same as not putting all your eggs in one basket. If C2 is detected and blocked, having a backup will allow operations to continue. C2 tiers generally fall into three categories: Interactive, Short Haul, and Long Haul. These are sometimes labeled as Tier 1, 2, or 3. There is nothing unique to each tier other than how they are used, and the deployment of redirectors is independent of the C2 tier.

The general rules to maintain multiple tiers are:

- Maintain discipline in each tier, and use it only for its intended purpose
- Only pass or establish new sessions down
    - Long Haul can pass only to Short Haul or Interactive
    - Short can pass to Interactive
    - Interactive can pass only to other interactive sessions
- For each tier, use a different profile—communication type, ports, protocols, callback times, etc.

Slow down callback time when not in use

Of course, there are exceptions to these rules. A Red Team must be flexible to achieve goals. If a rule is violated, be aware of the exposure risks before performing an action. For example, say that a Long Haul server dies after it is initially established. A Short or Interactive tier may be needed to reestablish the Long Haul.

Tiers and Their Uses

Interactive (Tier 3)
- Used for general commands, enumeration, scanning, data exfiltration, etc.
- This tier has the most interaction and is at the greatest risk of exposure
- Plan to lose access from communication failure, agent failure, or Blue Team actions
- Run enough interactive sessions to maintain access (Although interactive, this doesn't mean blasting the client with packets). Use good judgment to minimize interaction to just enough to perform an action

Short Haul (Tier 2)
- Used as a backup to reestablish interactive sessions.
- Use covert communications that blend in with the target.

- Slow callback times. Callback times in the 12–24 hr. range are common.

Long Haul (Tier 1)
- Used to reestablish short haul C2
- Slow callback times. Callback times of 24+ hours (often a few days) are common.

C2 Infrastructure Rules
- C2 servers do not directly communicate with targets
- Targets and C2 servers communicate through a redirector
- Tiers should be used for their intended purposes
    - Tier 1 – Low and slow, intended for long-term persistence
    - Tier 2 – Mid-speed communications, designed to reestablish interactive C2
    - Tier 3 – An Interactive tier designed to perform everyday commands near real time or as operationally required
    - New C2 must remain at the same tier or lower (never higher):
        - Tier 1 – Tier1 or Tier 2
        - Tier 2 – Tier 2 or Tier 3
        - Tier 3 – Tier 3

When can you violate a rule?
The only time C2 is passed is when C2 is initially established. An Interactive tier may be used to establish higher levels of access but is highly discouraged. There is a risk of exposing higher tiers. Caution must be used when setting up initial access.

Command and Control

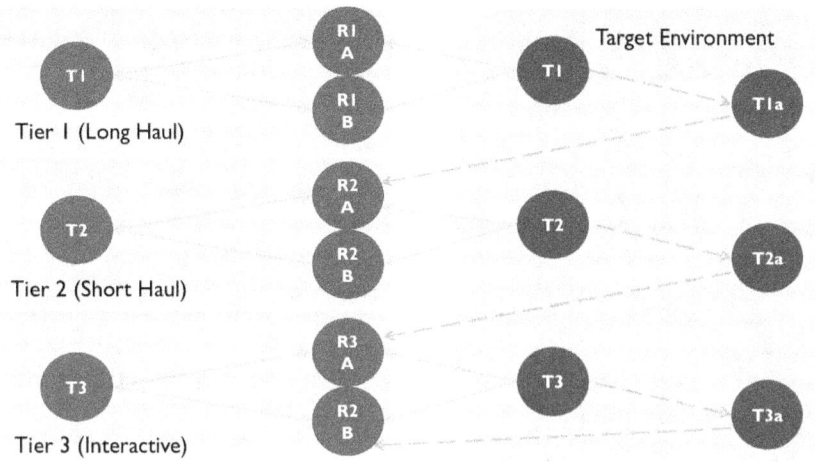

This diagram can help illustrate the tiers and the relationships of how to share information between each.

C2 Multi-tier Design

Designing a C2 infrastructure is one of the most critical tasks when planning a Red Team engagement. C2 infrastructure planning involves choosing the number and type of C2 servers, whether to use IP addresses or domain names, the C2 protocols, and how or if to use redirectors. The decision of each is directly related to a Red Team's goals. If a team is engaging a target in a full-scale Red Team operation, stealth and covert channels will be good choices.

Typical C2 Design for a Full-Scale Red Team Operation

- Three C2 servers with an Interactive tier, Short Haul server, and Long Haul server
- Multiple redirectors
- One or two carefully chosen domain names for each IP address (preferably with history and categorization)

- Direct communication between the target and C2 does not occur. All traffic pivots through a redirection server
- The use of common protocols on standard ports to blend (HTTP, HTTPS, SSH, DNS)
- Communications are encrypted

If a team is emulating a specific threat or trying to stimulate a Blue Team's response, stealth may not be as important.

Typical C2 Design for Emulating a Threat Designed to Stimulate Blue (Exercises)
- One or two C2 servers. All tiers are used for interaction with the target
- Redirectors are not in use
- IP addresses are used instead of domain names
- The target and C2 directly communicate
- The use of common protocols on standard or nonstandard ports (HTTP, HTTPS)
- Communications may or may not be encrypted

Domain Fronting

Domain Fronting is a technique developed to support the bypass of censorship by routing traffic through legitimate and highly trusted domains. There are many services that support Domain Fronting, including Google App Engine, Amazon CloudFront, and Microsoft Azure. How does this work? When the traffic is received by a provider's server, such as gmail.com, it is sent to an origin server, such as myapp.appspot.com. This is controlled based on a specified host header in the HTTP request. Either the origin server directly forwards traffic to a specified domain, which points to a threat-controlled C2 server, or a custom application proxies the request to complete the forwarding.

Note: Using domain fronting has been severely limited as organizations have actively been reducing the ability to use it. As of the writing of this book it is still an option, but like many techniques, will change over time.

References
1. Red Team Infrastructure Wiki, https://github.com/bluscreenofjeff/Red-Team-Infrastructure-Wiki#domain-fronting.
2. Domain Fronting Via Cloudfront Alternate Domains, https://www.mdsec.co.uk/2017/02/domain-fronting-via-cloudfront-alternate-domains/.
3. High-reputation Redirectors and Domain Fronting, https://blog.cobaltstrike.com/2017/02/06/high-reputation-redirectors-and-domain-fronting/.
4. Finding Frontable Domains, https://github.com/rvrsh3ll/FindFrontableDomains

Key Chapter Takeaways

Engagement execution involves all efforts from the end of planning to the start of culmination and reporting, including the build-out of infrastructure. The execution phase is simply the practical application of the "why" and "how" from planning.

Also remember:
- Good tradecraft is more valuable than any individual capability
- Sometimes the best way to exploit a system is to avoid using exploits
- A detailed C2 plan and defined infrastructure can be the difference between a successful and unsuccessful engagement
- Tools are enablers, nothing more
    - Know your tools and when to (or when not to) execute them
    - Ensure you understand why a tool is executed, what it does, and what indicators (or artifacts) it provides!
- Log, log, log!

Homework

1. Expand the data handling guide to include data repository and storage guidelines
2. Develop a data collection process and workflow for operators. Consider manual and automated collection options
3. Develop a tradecraft guidance guide
4. Develop a standard toolbox. Note: this is recommended but optional
5. Develop a command and control architecture and c2 deployment plan

Engagement Culmination

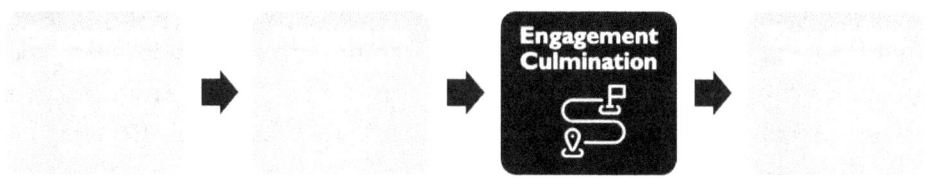

Following the execution phase, each engagement includes a series of activities required for a successful close-out, clean-up, and final reporting. This section walks through the steps needed to close out an engagement successfully.

Sanitization and Cleanup

All evidence of an engagement must be sanitized before Red Team departure. Any evidence describing the nature of the attacks, vulnerabilities, results, or other information must be entirely removed and destroyed. This clean-up includes tools and artifacts as well as reversing any modifications to security controls that could leave an environment less secure when an engagement ends.

In addition to system modifications, Red Teams may have the opportunity to modify or bypass security controls. If target system security controls were disabled or modified, they must be restored as soon as possible. These should be tracked with all other changes.

> **ROE is Law**
>
> The sanitization process must be documented in the ROE prior to engagement execution. This is the best way to ensure the clean up process is documented and, if followed, executed appropriately.

It is desired to have all exploits, toolkits, and persistence mechanisms have self-destruct code baked in as both time-based, to prevent execution outside the engagement window, and target-based to prevent exploitation outside the target environment. For items that do not have built-in self-destruct code, the Red Team should remove each individually and document the removal. When cleanup is not possible (communications lost, system taken offline, permission, etc.), the Red Team will alert the TA with the system name, IP address, directories, filenames, modification date, modifications made, tools left behind, or files modified. A change tracking log should be part of every engagement's required toolset (Note: if using the logging recommendations made earlier in the text, this tracking is captured in the log). Systems modifications should always be expected and planned as part of an engagement. These modifications are not only permanent changes such as dropped files or Windows registry modifications but also in memory processes. The following quick checklist will help an engagement lead remove all changes.

Engagement modification removal checklist

- Revert file system modifications
- Remove access mechanisms and backdoors
- Remove files dropped by an operator or operator's tools
- Ensure file artifacts generated by the mechanism are removed.
- Examine the entire system to confirm that the mechanism was not inadvertently copied or moved.
- Remove or restore Registry keys if used.
- Restore modified files.
- Remove or replace launch files with the originals.
- Examine startup scripts if used. Note that startup content may have changed.
- Remove execution mechanisms.
- Remove the installation mechanism.
- Copy log files generated by the mechanism to the Red Team repository and remove them from the target system.

- Remove C2 persistence mechanisms
- Terminate C2 channels
- Continue connection monitoring for stray or missed mechanisms.
- Repeat the process for strays.
- Provide a list of all artifacts, names, hashes, locations, and their cleanup status to the TA.

> **Consider This**
>
> Sometimes the target organization may want specific artifacts (perhaps all) left on the network for training or tool and processing tuning purposes.
>
> This must be approved and documented prior to engagement closure. A list of all artifacts and modifications must still be provided to the target's designated TA.

Operator Log Verification

Each operator must verify the completion of his or her operator logs prior to the end of an engagement. Each must also check that all operator logs, data collected via automation, target data, and screenshots have been appropriately named and stored in the engagement data folder.

> **Consider This**
>
> It's best to perform operator log completion throughout the engagement. An engagement lead who has operators ensure logs are complete before the end of each day will significantly reduce missing logs or critical screenshots.

Upon the notification of completion by the operators, the Red Team lead must review the consolidation. If the lead is satisfied that the data is complete, they should create a hashed compressed archive of all data. Copies made of the archive should be stored in an approved location. This archive is can be an encrypted removable media device that maintains controlled access or any approved location for storage of this sensitive data.

The Red Team Lead is ultimately responsible for the acceptance, review, and consolidation of operator logs and all data. It is highly recommended that the Red Team Lead periodically check the team's repository during engagement execution to ensure that records are being completed, data is being appropriately named and stored, and logs reflect adherence to the ROE.

Log Completion Checklist

- Ensure completion of all operator logs
- Ensure consolidation of all logs
- Ensure consolidation of data collected automatically
- Ensure consolidation of target data
- Red Team Lead review and acceptance
- Archive (Tar/Zip) and hash all data

Pre-Report Briefings

It is recommended to perform a closeout brief following the final day of the engagement. This brief will likely not include much of the detail in the final report; however, it should allow the Red Team to provide the target with a high-level overview of the access gained correlated to the significant observations of the engagement, general feedback, and general recommendations.

Executive Outbrief

At the end of an engagement's execution, a target organization typically needs (and often warrants) a summary of the event. Waiting for a final report can keep the target out of the loop for too long. If logging and data collection were performed correctly (as it should have been), this would not be a difficult task.

The first post-engagement meeting is usually the executive outbrief. An executive brief is typically performed soon after execution completes (within one or two days following execution). This meeting is tailored toward management and should include key personnel from the target organization. This meeting should not only include information security management but organizational management as well. The outcome of a Red Team engagement may impact how an organization operates in the future, potentially requiring funding to pursue mitigations or staffing modifications. Management awareness and buy-in are critical if Red Team results will be used to improve an organization's security stance to defend and respond to a threat.

The executive outbrief should focus on the big picture of the event and is best portrayed as a chronological story of critical steps and observations. The story and actions will become the attack narrative in the final report. At this point, the final report and analysis are not complete, but management is looking for quick answers. If obvious issues were identified, they could be highlighted in the brief. It should be pointed out that the final report may contain observations that will not be discovered until all information has been analyzed.

> **Consider This**
>
> Most executive suites and senior managers aren't as interested in the technical details of the engagement. They are more commonly interested in the impacts to business functions, production, and reputation.
>
> Attempt to correlate each major action or milestone to the business aspects impacted. If possible, estimating total costs (including lost revenue, time, remediation, capability, etc.) facilitates executive understanding of the impacts and reinforces interaction.

Executive Outbrief Checklist

- Occurs immediately after engagement execution
- Include organizational management (decision makers)
- Include key information security and technical staff
- Focus on the chronological summary of observations (story of the event)
- Highlight critical observations
- Inform the audience that this brief is merely a summary. The final report will contain all event details

Optional

- Include additional information security or technical staff
- Include critical system experts
- Include legal staff

Technical Outbrief

A technical outbrief (or tech-on-tech briefing) is extremely valuable to the organization, to the Defensive/Blue Team, and to the Red Team itself.

These technical exchanges do not always occur but are too valuable to ignore and should be a required step for every engagement.

The tech-on-tech is a bi-directional technical exchange of information between the Red Team, the Blue Team, and the organization. During this exchange, both the Red and the defensive elements provide a highly detailed, step-by-step technical review of the actions and results (including all associated details) of the engagement. This is where training and education meet and is one of the most valuable opportunities for all parties to learn. More often than not, the defenders discover that they had very little insight into Red Team actions on the network. The tech-on-tech allows both sides to participate in a detailed walkthrough conjoined with a question and answer session.

The occurrence of the tech-on-tech is often more useful to those who will implement mitigations or changes driven by red team activity than the final report. While the process is quite simple, the value is unsurpassed. A few tech-on-tech actions/roles have been identified below to give you a better understanding of what should take place.

Tech-on-Tech Briefing Checklist and Agenda Planning

The Red Team:

- Explains Red TTPs and intended IOCs.
- Explains their initial thought process for meeting the engagement objectives.
- Steps through Red actions and associated activity/commands. (This occurs simultaneously with the defender walkthrough.)
- Describes why those actions were executed. (What lead to each specific action?)
- Provides the results of each action and how that action enabled the next.

- Provides recommendations or techniques that would limit each threat action.

The defensive team:

- Has the opportunity to ask the how and why.
- Explains the process for securing and defending the environment.
- Identifies any alerts, triggers, or anomalies within the environment during the engagement.
- Steps through the Blue actions in response to Red Team activity. (This occurs simultaneously with the Red Team walkthrough.)
- Identifies how Red Team activity could have been detected, prevented, or leveraged (Red Team input is usually key during this discussion period).
- Provides feedback on the Red Team actions and recommendations.
- Uses tech-on-tech information to perform a post-engagement analysis prior to the receipt of the official report.

Responding to negative organizational feedback during briefings

Inevitably, a Red Team will be challenged in their observations. A Red Team must be prepared to respond to negative questions or comments, such as "We gave you access," "A bad guy would never do that," or "How is that fair?". These comments are all too common and typically come from organizations that are immature or uninformed about threats and security.

In order to respond appropriately, a Red Team must remain professional and conduct a high-quality engagement. Red Teaming can generate stress and cause people to become defensive, both personally and professionally.

A Red Team should not boast or belittle the target's staff during a briefing or in a report. A Red Team that tells the story of an engagement with simple facts can convey a strong message without blame. Even if an organization did poorly, the facts would be more than enough to get the point across. Remember, a Red Team's job is not to demonstrate how elite their hacking skills are but to exercise a threat scenario that allows an organization to learn and improve their security. A Red Team's story should convey the significant failures that led to a successful compromise.

A good rule of practice is non-attribution, or not attributing failures to specific people. Many organizations blame security failures on certain individuals instead of recognizing organizational gaps or failures. Placing blame on individuals seems to present an easy fix but rarely improves security. Blaming Bob in accounting for clicking a phishing email is not why all intellectual property was stolen.

On occasion, a Red Team may be presented with an unusually hostile person or possibly a hostile technical team. In these scenarios, diffusing hostilities becomes just as important as the information being conveyed; otherwise, the information may not be ingested as intended. The Red Team can use three simple questions to begin diffusing the situation.

Questions to Defuse Hostile Response to Red Team Activity

1. Did the action operate within scope?

   A well-planned engagement will have a well-defined scope. If all activities operate within scope, all activities are acceptable.

   In cases where a Red Team is provided with information, state this upfront when describing the scenario.

   List the assumptions to help ensure that the audience agrees with the assumptions or, at a minimum, understand why specific actions were taken.

2. Did the action operate within the Rules of Engagement?

   The Rules of Engagement dictate everything about how an action will or will not be performed. The ROE must be followed. Violating rules is a quick way for a Red Team to lose the trust and confidence of the organization. As with operating in scope, if the Rules of Engagement were not violated, the action is acceptable.

3. Has the action been performed in a real-world attack?

   If an action or technique has been used in the real world, it has validity. Organizations can quickly become skeptical of theoretical attacks. Being able to tie an action to a known technique or threat will help validate its authenticity.

Key Chapter Takeaways

The culmination phase is a major milestone in a Red Team engagement. All activity is complete, and data or logs are finalized. If data validation is not complete, there is a serious risk to developing a quality report. This is the last opportunity to ensure logs are complete, screenshots exist, and the engagement story can be told.

Culmination is the first official time the target organization receives information on the outcome of an engagement. The success or failure of an engagement often lies in the quality of the briefing performed in this phase.

If performed correctly, the Red Team lead should have everything needed to begin developing a quality, professional report.

Homework

- Develop an engagement system modification tracking document
- Develop a sanitization and cleanup tracking document
- Ensure operator log verification is included in the engagement methodology or workflow
- Develop an agenda template for executive outbriefs
- Develop an agenda template for tech-on-tech outbriefs

Engagement Reporting

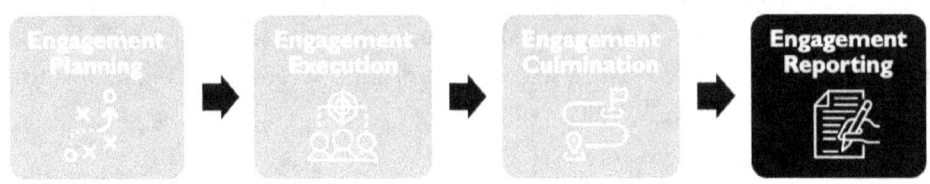

Reports are the final product and the only evidence of an engagement. The reporting phase is a critical aspect of a Red Team engagement. Reports should enable the organization to replicate the actions and results of the Red Team and are the last form of evidence that can be analyzed and used to provide a base for improving security. They must be included as a final delivery for an engagement. Some teams (especially internal teams) often do not produce formal reports. Some only provide a list of findings and label as a report. While this is acceptable (assuming some detailed deliverable is produced), it is strongly encouraged to develop a formal reporting process using a standard template. This process ensures consistency and completeness in delivering a final product following an engagement.

> **Rules Regarding Data Collection and Reporting**
>
> 1. If an action is not logged, it did not happen.
> 2. If there is no report, there was no engagement

Reports not only document the activity that occurred during a specific engagement but also provide an excellent reference that can be used as a reliable roadmap to plan and design other or future engagements. Many engagements share similar approaches and goals. As the number of reports grows, they can be analyzed together to understand common patterns and risks shared by various environments. These can be used to understand how threats succeed or fail when facing varying levels of defense.

Attack Flow Diagrams

Everyone has heard that an image is worth a thousand words. The same applies when generating reports. This is especially true in those containing complex threads and activities. Red Teaming is about understanding a threat's impact of actions against a target. Although this is documented in logs and eventually written as observations, a visual diagram is extremely valuable and one of the most effective ways to describe and highlight key activities and observations.

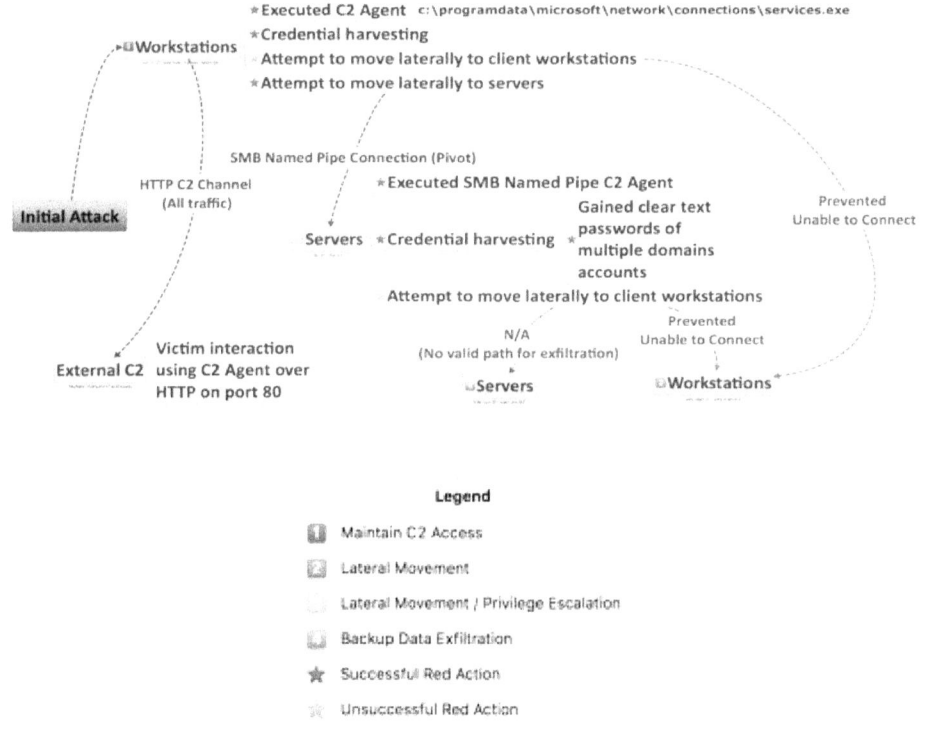

The diagram above is a sanitized example of a real Red Team engagement leveraging a simple assumed breach model. This engagement was used to train a new red team using a small, simplified engagement. The engagement goals included the following:

- Train and expose a new red team to the red team processes
- Measure the ability a threat has to move laterally
- Measure the defender's ability to detect C2 traffic and binaries
- Measure the ability to perform and subsequently detect critical data exfiltration

This Red Team engagement was designed as C2 training for a new Red Team and to educate a Blue Team on threat techniques. The Red Team designed and staged Command and Control with specific IOCs and threat objectives using a threat profile to document the threat design. The diagram highlights the actions, successes, and failures of the Red Team and was created using the commercial mind mapping software XMind (http://www.xmind.net/) but could have easily been created in a number of other diagraming tools.

A properly designed diagram can be used solely to present a Red Team engagement. The power of an image is truly immense. Diagrams are not required but are highly encouraged.

Consider This

The authors of this book often only use diagrams to drive executive or technical briefings verses using a long text driven document or PowerPoint presentation. Graphical presentations are a great way to convey the complex actions of a Red Team engagement.

Observations vs. Findings

The Red Team engagement report can be quite different than reports generated in penetration tests or vulnerability assessments. Engagement goals and associated impacts are the foundational data points that directly feed a Red Team report. As previously discussed, Red Team engagements are highly scenario-focused. This leads to a story-driven report that contains the Red Team's story (or flow) and their ability to execute or meet their goals.

Penetration testing or vulnerability assessment reports focus on findings. For example, a penetration test may discover a weak password policy that leaves an organization susceptible to a brute force attack, or missing patches allowed the exploitation of end-user workstations. These findings are typically mapped to some security control or policy. Perhaps these findings would lead to the recommendations of modifying the password policy to require longer passwords, implementing two-factor authentication, and ensuring that the patching policy is being followed. These are important findings to discover, but these fall more in the line of security housekeeping and attack surface reduction.

Red Team engagements have much different goals than other security tests. The methods to describe goals in a Red Team report are better represented as observations rather than discrete findings. For example, an out-of-date system may have flaws that allow an operator to compromise a workstation. This provides command and control and is used to perform situational awareness on the target's organization's assets. An operator continues to explore and move through the target's network and eventually steals proprietary data as a planned goal. The technical flaw is important and should be documented but is only one of a series of steps. This series of steps can be used to detail the observation a threat has regarding freedom of movement.

> **Example Observation**
>
> The red team was able to move freely through the target's network with little to no resistance. The initial compromised host provided the initial stepping stone but was soon abandoned once freedom of movement was established. The red team did not observe any preventive or detective controls that would indicate the organization was aware of the threat activity. This freedom of movement was key in providing the ability to exfiltrate sensitive data from the target.

The Red Team is driven by goals intended to stimulate or measure not only technical flaws but security operations as a whole. This includes people, processes, and technology. A Red Team report uses a story-based format where observations rather than of findings are listed.

Risk Rating and Metrics

Most security tests include a risk rating with a finding. A common scale uses risk matrix diagram composed of Impact vs. Likelihood in High, Medium or Low assignments. It is most often represented in a 3x3 square diagram. While this may give a general idea of risk, it is often too arbitrary and subjective. The values chosen are at the discretion of the report writers. Unless the target organization is included in the rating decision, these ratings include only the security tester perspective. These types of ratings work well for vulnerability assessments, where individual vulnerabilities are the primary goal and can be assigned associated CVE scores. It can also work for penetration tests when measuring and validating levels of exploitability is the primary goal.

These types of ratings can be used in Red Team reports; however, they are not appropriate for the observation methodology. Let's consider this example. If a Red Team had a goal of stealing proprietary organizational data, the observation write-up would describe how and where the data was taken and the volume of data acquired. This is difficult to summarize into a single dot on an impact vs. likelihood risk matrix. Consider another option, using the metrics of Red Team goals. Red Team goals were discussed earlier in the book. These goals have associated metrics in the form of questions. Instead of rating risk using a subjective scale, a narrative that answers the questions can describe the risk. This does not assign a High or Low value but provides an organization with information that can be used to determine the level of action needed.

If an Impact vs. Likelihood risk matrix diagram is required, include both the Red Team goal narrative and the vulnerability risk matrix. Remember, Red Teaming focuses on goals and not vulnerabilities. Vulnerabilities will be discovered during a red team engagement and can be documented using the traditional risk matrix grid in a secondary findings section of the report.

Risk Matrices Comparison

Risk matrices are a great way to add a visual element to a report to provide additional context and understanding. This matrix is commonly used to estimate the degree of severity and the probability or level of some impact to a specific discrete vulnerability or finding

3 × 3 risk matrix example

The 3x3 risk matrix is arguably the most common in security reports. It is relatively simple and provides nine possible levels to assign risk. This type of rating is highly subjective. It is challenging for a security tester (vulnerability, penetration, or red team) to accurately rate impact or probability in terms of risk to operations. This leads to ratings focused at the technical level. While this is useful, it doesn't always provide leadership the view needed to make an informed decision on applying mitigations using their limited resources.

		LOW	MEDIUM	HIGH
LIKELIHOOD	HIGH	MEDIUM	HIGH	HIGH
	MEDIUM	LOW	MEDIUM	HIGH
	LOW	LOW	LOW	MEDIUM
		IMPACT		

Likelihood: The probability that an event will occur:

- Low – Not likely to occur
- Medium – May occur
- High – Probably will occur

Impact: The expected result of an event (degree of injury, property damage, or other mission-impairing factors) measured as:

- Low – Limited impact on operations
- Medium – Noticeable impact on operations
- High – Significant impact on operations

5 × 5 risk matrix example

The 5x5 risk matrix is an extended version of the 3x3. The usage is the same but provides a bit more granularity. This can help fine-tune the rating but suffers from similar limitations. It does offer a method to view risk in terms of operations instead of discrete vulnerabilities. The version presented has been adopted and modified from the U.S. Army[21] and NIST[22] to focus on operation impact instead of mission impact.

PROBABILITY		NEGLIGIBLE	MARGINAL	MODERATE	CRITICAL	CATASTROPHIC
	Frequent	LOW	MEDIUM	HIGH	VERY HIGH	VERY HIGH
	Likely	LOW	LOW	MEDIUM	HIGH	VERY HIGH
	Occasional	VERY LOW	LOW	LOW	MEDIUM	HIGH
	Seldom	VERY LOW	VERY LOW	LOW	LOW	MEDIUM
	Unlikely	VERY LOW	VERY LOW	VERY LOW	VERY LOW	LOW
		\multicolumn{5}{c}{SEVERITY}

Probability: The likeliness that an event will occur:

- Frequent – Occurs often
- Likely – Occurs several times in x period
- Occasional – Occurs sporadically
- Seldom – Unlikely but could occur
- Unlikely – Probably will not occur

Severity: The expected result of an event (degree of injury, property damage, or other mission-impairing factors) measure as:

---

[21] "Risk Management - Army Publishing Directorate - Army.mil." 14 Apr. 2014, https://armypubs.army.mil/epubs/DR_pubs/DR_a/pdf/web/atp5_19.pdf.
[22] "NIST Special Publication 800-30 Revision 1, Guide for ...." https://nvlpubs.nist.gov/nistpubs/Legacy/SP/nistspecialpublication800-30r1.pdf.

- Catastrophic – Direct impact, usually of long duration if not permanent
- Critical – Significant impact: stops or halts operation
- Moderate – Noticeable loss: reduces/slows operation/production
- Marginal – Limited loss: noticed but does not halt operation
- Negligible – Some loss: unnoticed if not monitored closely

The key in these matrices construct is vulnerability. As stated several times throughout this book, Red Teaming is not vulnerability focused. Given that thought process, a Red Team's engagement should be constructed as a narrative of threat actions. Below are a few questions that can help determine the impact and shape Red Team's goals. Refer to the Red Team Goals section of this book for more details. These questions should directly reflect the goals created during engagement planning.

Questions to consider when developing red team goals:

- What ability does an adversary have to access common areas?
- What ability does an adversary have to access restricted areas?
- Can an adversary use gained access to enable electronic capabilities?
- What impacts can an adversary have with gained access?
- Can an adversary access key/critical systems?
- What impacts can an adversary have on a key/critical system?
- What ability does an adversary have to move through a network freely?
- How long can an adversary live on target without discovery?
- What actions are required to trigger a detection/response?

These questions shift focus on measuring or understanding the ability a threat has to perform some action or the ability the defense has on impacting the threat. This leads to the need of an alternate means of providing risk metrics.

Three-tiered categorization

Chris Crowley[23] has proposed a simple yet highly effective concept for categorization using only three tiers. While this tiered structure was intended to be applied to security operations, it can be applied to virtually any concept.

A benefit to this model is the categories focus on the ability to mitigate rather than risk. By nature, this provides an actionable plan to implement improvements. Let's review and understand this concept by starting with the tier categories. Each tier is defined based on the relative ease of applying a mitigation to the observation or finding.

Tiered Matrix

Category	Rating
1	The correction is readily available in the environment but has not been implemented or applied.
2	The correction or mitigation is readily available in the environment or public, but something such as policy, procedure, politics, contracts, training, etc. prevents implementation or application.
3	The correction or mitigation is not readily available in any industry or sector. Research or additional effort is required to investigate to determine a correction or mitigation plan.

---

[23] "Chris Crowley (@CCrowMontance) | author of SANS MGT535, MGT517, and SOC-Class." https://twitter.com/ccrowmontance?lang=en.

Example Diagram Summarizing Categories

3.1 Observation: Client-to-Client lateral movement
Rating: Category 2

During the engagement, the Red Team was able to move laterally permissive client-to-client communications. This allowed the Red Team to pivot toward sensitive systems and enable greater access to target their goals.

Recommendation:
In general clients have no business communicating with other clients. When lateral movement is permissive, a threat can use this to move freely through out a network ...

Example snippet from a report showing how to use category rating

Author's Thoughts

Very few things should be labeled 3. There's almost always an acceptable mitigation/workaround.

Many will likely be labeled 2. This should be cause for policy or process change and could be used to justify additional training.

Anything labeled 1 should be of great concern to the organization, division, or management. Often indicates a lack of effort.

It is important to note that this method of categorization requires open and effective communication between the Red Team and the organization. Internal Red Teams may have the organizational knowledge and experience required to categorize their observations. However, as most Red Teams (internal or external) are not typically part of the business function being assessed, require a collaborative review and discussion of each observation.

During Red Team reporting, this method can be used in conjunction with the Pyramid of Pain to illustrate how a specific correction impacts a threat's ability to perform nefarious actions. This knowledge can, in turn, be leveraged to create a prioritization of corrections or organizational modifications.

Pyramid of Pain

Security operations do not need a list of patches or misconfiguration flaws as the highlight of mitigations or recommendations. Yes, these should be included in the report. However, it is much more beneficial to provide security operations with a list of actions, processes, procedures, etc. that would make a threat's ability to operate (move, gather data, and cause impact) much more difficult. A great way to both describe and illustrate this concept is the Pyramid of Pain.

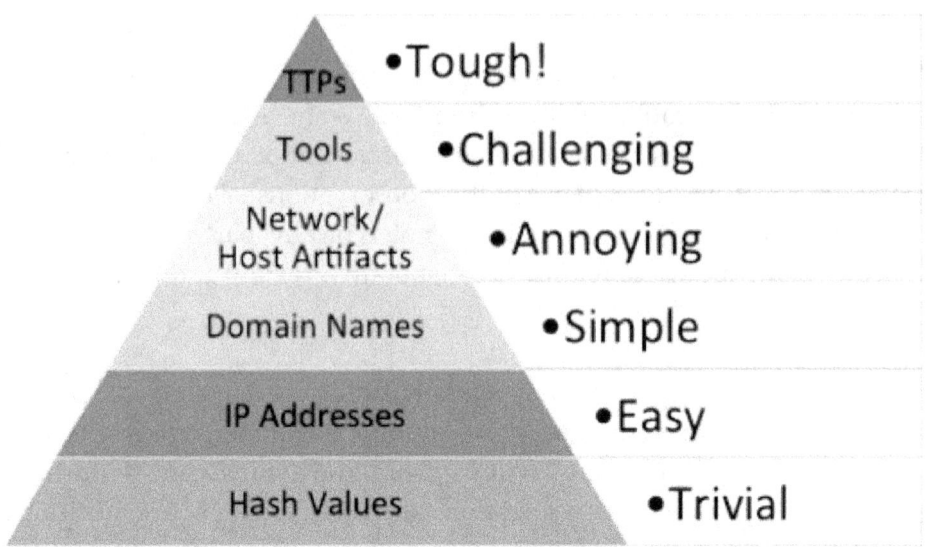

The Pyramid of Pain[24] was created and described by David Bianco in 2013 and revised later in 2014. The pyramid describes types of indicators that may be used to detect threat activities and how much pain will be caused (to the threat) if a Blue Team is able to deny a threat the ability to perform actions that generate those IOCs. What does this mean in terms of a Red Team engagement? Red Teams generate artifacts during an engagement. A Red Team can use the concept of the Pyramid of Pain to measure where they fit on this chart during an assessment. In other words, how much pain is Blue causing Red.

When a Blue Team is measured against the actions of a threat instead of against how well they detect malware, configure their firewalls, or implements a password policy, they are measured against threat techniques. This includes known, unknown, and even zero-day attacks. Decomposing threats into their actions provide defenders a manageable way to understand the effectiveness of their defensive strategy. Blue Teams

---

[24] "Enterprise Detection & Response: The ...." http://detect-respond.blogspot.com/2013/03/the-pyramid-of-pain.html.

can become more effective and better protect against any threat instead of defending against a single piece of malware.

A Blue Team Perspective

Detection in Depth

Detection Engineering (the process of creating detection logic for attacker activity) is an often misunderstood discipline. It is common to see these "detections" labeled as good or bad, but detection logic isn't inherently either. The misunderstanding tends to occur when someone's expectations of specific logic don't align with reality. To be successful in detection, it is important to build a detection mesh that combines precise indicators with low false-positive expectations (signatures) with broad indicators with low false-negative expectations (behavioral detections). I refer to this concept as Detection in Depth. This approach ensures that analysts can rely on high signal detection of known bad activity, while also expecting that the mesh will stand up to evasion attempts.

- Jared Atkinson, Microsoft MVP, @jaredcatkinson
  Introducing the Funnel of Fidelity -
  https://posts.specterops.io/introducing-the-funnel-of-fidelity-b1bb59b04036

What are some examples of defensible actions that would make a threat's ability to operate difficult?

Defensive Action	Description
Prevent client-to-client communication	Preventing these communications limits a threat's ability to move freely throughout the network, reduces the likelihood of privileged

	account discovery, forces an increase in time and effort (more activities and artifacts), and ,therefore, can increase the defender's ability to detect.
Prevent server-to-client communication	Assuming the network has prevented client-to-client communications, the only option a threat has is to attempt access to a server, but cannot communicate server to the client.
Block outbound server communications	There are very few instances where a server needs to communicate with a system external to the network. These are exceptions and should be managed to allow only connections to the required external asset or IP and allow only the use of required ports and protocols.
Clear cached administrative credentials	Cached credential discovery is a common and primary method in which threats escalate privileges.
Reset the KRBTGT Account	Reset the KRBTGT account twice within a limited time-frame followed by the changing of all administrative credentials. These resets limit a threat's ability to maintain access after credential changes.
Perform a sensitive items review	Perform frequent search and discovery activities for critical items stored across organizational assets (Passwords, Configs,

	Privacy of Information Act (PIA) data, Intellectual Property, etc.)
Block and Disable non-required ports, protocols, and services (PPS)	Both internal and external systems and network devices should disable and block PPS that aren't required for the network. Limit PPS to only what is required for each specific system.
Implement separation of accounts and privileges	Users should be limited to only what is required to perform daily tasks. Standard users often do not require elevated privileges on a daily basis. In rare scenarios where a user needs elevation often, require the use of a secondary account with only the access required and no external communications ability.
Ensure group permissions are appropriately identified and mapped	This recommendation has multiple applications; however, the main focus is nested groups and permissions.
Implement Microsoft Local Administrator Password Solution (LAPS)	No two local accounts have the same password. A client-side component generates a random password, updates the LAPS password on the Active Directory computer account, and sets the password locally.

Multi-Factor Authentication	Additional security control and protection that requires more than one authenticator or authentication factor for successful authentication.
Application Whitelisting	Implement Application Whitelisting only after all of the prior recommendations have been implemented.

This list is comprised of list of preventable controls (Mitigation Strategies Part 1[25] and Part 2[26]) and is a great list of starter techniques a Red Team can use to apply Red Team techniques that directly measures security operations ability to detect and response to threat techniques.

Attack Narrative

The Attack Narrative section of the report contains the observations made during a Red Team engagement. It is the written version of the attack diagram. These are typically written in chronological order and follows the execution flow of an engagement. Key observations that a Red Team uses to achieve its goals must be documented. This includes all major successful and failed steps taken while working toward a goal. Threat profiles or other indicators that Blue can use during post-analysis should be included. The end of a Red Team engagement can be the beginning of post-forensic analysis or hunt team engagement. Blue teams that take advantage of the IOCs listed in the report after an engagement through post-analysis can

---

[25] "Threat Mitigation Strategies - Threatexpress." https://threatexpress.com/blogs/2018/threat-mitigation-strategies-observations-recommendations/..
[26] "Threat Mitigation Strategies Part 2 - Threatexpress." 15 May. 2018, https://threatexpress.com/blogs/2018/threat-mitigation-strategies-technical-recommendations-and-info-part-2/.

use this to find blind spots or to tune security tools to better protect against threats by comparing what was discovered against what was not.

Types of Observations that Should Be Documented

Observation to be Documented	Description
Key actions that led from initial access to the final goal	Actions that describe how access was gained as various phases of the engagement. Include • Initial access • Lateral movement • Privilege escalation
Command and Control	Overview of C2 design and architecture. Include • Network information (IP addresses, domain name, ports, protocols, etc.) • Include agent information (binaries, scripts, locations, and Registry changes) • Include persistence methods
Reconnaissance actions	Steps taken to perform reconnaissance or situational awareness. Include • Techniques used that help identify potential indicators • Include key pieces of information

	gathered
Interesting observations that assisted the red team during the engagement	Operators often take advantage of unique situations to support an engagement. This is often non-technical in nature. Observations related to people, processes, and technology should be documented. Include • Logic flaws found in the environment • Response (or lack of) from defenders
Interesting observations that may be of concern but that are not directly related to the engagement	Engagement offer a unique view to a range of systems. Operators often find interesting paths or other observations that may or may not have been explored. These should be documented.

A single observation should Include the following elements (a complete example is available on the companion website)

- Observation title
- A narrative description
- Technical details
    - Source/destination IP addresses
    - Tools or techniques
    - Results (Including impacts)
- Screenshots

Internal Enumeration and Lateral Movement

After the initial compromise, internal focus shifted to internal network and the environment.tgt Windows Domain.

Environment.tgt Windows Domain Enumeration

The domain was enumerated using Windows PowerShell and built-in Windows tools from a limited domain user account.

The following items were enumerated:
- Domain Users, Computers, Groups, Trusts, Password Policy
- SYSVOL Policies and Scripts
- File Servers and Shares
- Search for Group Policy Preferences Passwords
- Search for Logged on Domain Administrator accounts
- Search for Service Accounts SPN Records

... (TRUNCATED)

Service Kerberos Ticket Granting Service (TGS) tickets for all the service accounts installed on the domain were extracted. A weakness in the Windows implementation of Kerberos allows offline brute force password cracking against these service tickets. The tickets were loaded on a dedicated password cracking system.

```
$ proxychains python GetUserSPNs.py                    -request -dc-ip
ProxyChains-3.1 (http://proxychains.sf.net)
Impacket v0.9.15-dev - Copyright 2002-2016 Core Security Technologies

Password:
|S-chain|-<>-           :9050-<>-        :389-<>-OK
ServicePrincipalName              Name              MemberOf

MSSQLSvc/
MSSQLSvc/
```

... (TRUNCATED)

Server Exploitation and Privilege Escalation

The account "environment\svcservice" was successfully cracked from the SPN tickets found earlier. The account was not found to be a domain administrator, but was found to be administrator on "Server". Using the cracked credential, SMB was used to pivot to the server through existing C2.

... (TRUNCATED)

Example Observation

Where to Include Findings and Recommendations

Although a report is focused on the attack diagram and narrative, flaws will be identified and should be reported in a findings section of the report. Findings should be a list of critical issues that helped the Red Team with their success in achieving goals. These should include traditional findings, such as lack of patching, weak passwords, or other common flaws.

Recommendations of mitigations are typically generic at this phase. In order to enhance recommendations and provide mitigation advice that directly focuses on the target organization, there must be a collaboration with the Red Team and the target organization to determine the root cause of the security failures. Unfortunately, this does not always occur. Many Red Teams provide a list of recommendations, and these are taken as ground truth. Red teams should encourage a proper risk assessment to be performed regarding the recommended mitigations. Red teams only provide one side of the risk equation. Organizations that use a report to conduct their own root cause analysis are often better off and implement more robust improvement to their security operations.

> **Focus Point**
>
> Although Findings and recommendations are not the focus of a Red Team engagement or always requested, they should always be included in an appendix.

After observations are analyzed and understood, the Red Team has an understanding of how the defense fared against the attack, but this understanding is often one-sided. I can be difficult to provide exact recommendation or remediations. It can be beneficial to provide a relationship instead of a direct recommendation. A relationship that gives an overall picture of an engagement will help describe how improvements will increase security.

 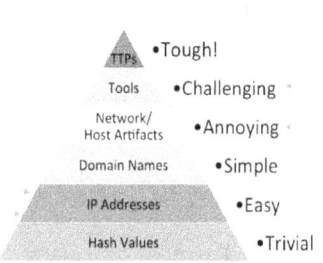 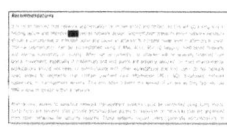

The details in this example are not important. The mapping of observation to recommendation in relationship to the pyramid of pain is the focus. The left of the image shows the red team's observations mapped to the defense's ability to impact the threat actions. This is currently at Easy. The right of the image describes the issue and provides a recommendation. If the target organization implements the recommendation, the Red Team estimates the defensive posture and impact to the threat. In this case, to challenging or annoying.

Reporting does not explicitly need to display this diagram, but the concept should be understood in the report context. Note, as with the attack diagram, images assist understanding. Including visuals, along with text, dramatically increases the chances of ingestion and application.

183

Key Chapter Takeaways

A Red Team engagement report is the final and only piece of evidence of a red team engagement. These reports can be quite different than other security reports. Reports should focus on the attack narrative and highlight the key observations made by operators during engagement execution.

Applying a risk rating can be difficult as red team observations are often one-sided. Consider applying ratings by directly working with a risk team or individuals from the security operations team. Use these tips to apply a rating in cases where the red team will provide a rating.

- Use an observation section to support the attack narrative
- Use a findings section to track and define technical flaws
- Apply the three-tiered rating technique for observations
- Apply a 5x5 rating techniques for technical findings

Homework

1. Develop a custom report template
2. Create a collection of observations to enable consistent wording when reporting on repeated observations in the attack narrative.
3. Create a findings section to track technical findings (similar to a penetration test report).
4. Develop an attack flow diagram template.
5. Develop an attack flow narrative template.

Summary

Red Teaming is the process of using well-defined Tactics, Techniques, and Procedures (TTPs) to emulate a real-world threat with the goals of training and measuring the effectiveness of the people, processes, and technology used to defend an environment.

Emphasis should be placed on the impacts of threat operations vs. the enabling vulnerabilities. Vulnerabilities will be discovered and leveraged; however, the weaknesses found are a byproduct of a Red Team engagement, not the focus. Red Team results should be much more than just a list of identified flaws. They provide a deeper understanding of how an organization would perform against an actual threat. A Red Team's real value is assisting a target identify administrative, technical, and procedural controls that directly limit a threat's ability to cause negative impacts. Even when vulnerable to the latest "zero-day vulnerability." Consequently, Operational Impacts provide real insight into the ability security operations has to protect, detect, respond, or recover from a variety of threats.

Did you notice engagement planning was quite a bit longer than execution, culmination, and reporting? There is a method to that madness. Engagement Planning is crucial to manage potential engagement risks effectively, successfully execute desired goals and objectives, and providing the information required to improve both organizational and defensive capabilities. In short, it is nearly impossible to conduct a professional and successful engagement without fully understanding the goals and scope, understanding the resources required to execute, and creating a solid plan. Likewise, effective planning dramatically increases the speed and accuracy of both engagement culmination and reporting. The importance of engagement planning cannot be stressed enough.

Deliverables (Reports) enable the organization to replicate the actions and results of the Red Team. They are the last form of evidence that can be analyzed and used to provide a base for improving security. They must be included as a final delivery for an engagement.

Finally, we would like to stress our common mantra. "If there is no log, there was no action. If there is no report, there was no engagement". Red Team operators and leads should take this to heart and encourage each other to document their actions properly.

---

http://redteam.guide

Don't forget to visit the companion website, http://redteam.guide for additional information, Red Team templates, and other guides.

Conclusion

We want to thank you for taking the time to read this content. Of course, reading is only one step in your efforts. It is also essential to absorb, process, and understand the lessons and concepts as presented. If you didn't while reading, we recommend working through the homework assignments. The best way to learn and improve upon these concepts is to implement and practice them.

It has taken years of research, experimentation (a.k.a trial-and-error), and execution to discern what elements should and should not be part of this text. Our goal was to provide practical guidance to assist you, or your team, in the development, management, and execution of a professional Red Team. Volumes upon volumes could be written on each individual topic; however, we have attempted to write to the 80/20 rule. Eighty (80) percent of what you see, hear, and experience is the least valuable information. This text covers what we believe to be the twenty (20) percent of Red Team Development and Operations that has the most value. It will not only make you a better Red Teamer, but it should also provide a means to streamline your efforts and alleviate your work-load. In the end, improving (making things better) and enjoying yourself in the process is what counts the most. Again, thank you!

Appendix A: Example Templates

Templates and examples can be found on the companion website, http://redteam.guide.

Appendix B: Thought Exercises

Adversarial Mindset Challenge

Description
In the exercise, you'll quickly complete a series of puzzle challenges designed to encourage critical thinking in a short time frame. This is designed to be a fun way to begin understanding the skills needed to plan and execute a red team plan.

Instructions
Follow each puzzle's instructions
Set a time and complete the puzzles within 5 minutes.

STOP here and prepare to begin when ready

9 Dot Puzzle

Instructions:

Placing your pen on the page only once, draw four straight lines that pass through all nine dots without lifting the pen from the page.

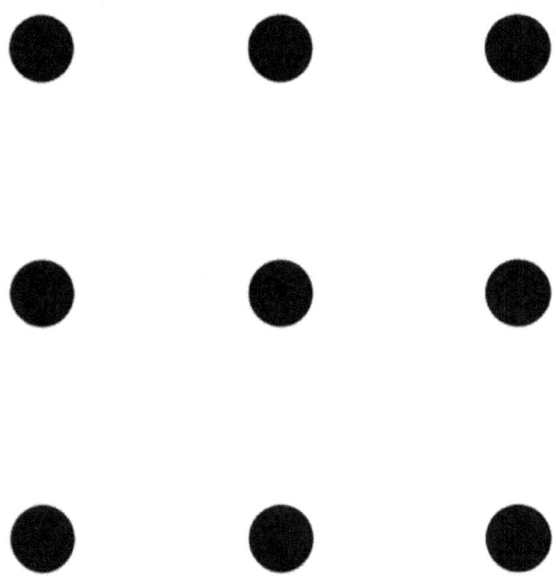

Maze Challenge

Instructions:
Draw a line from the laptop to the data center.

Triangle Puzzle

Instructions:
Count the triangles. How many are shown?

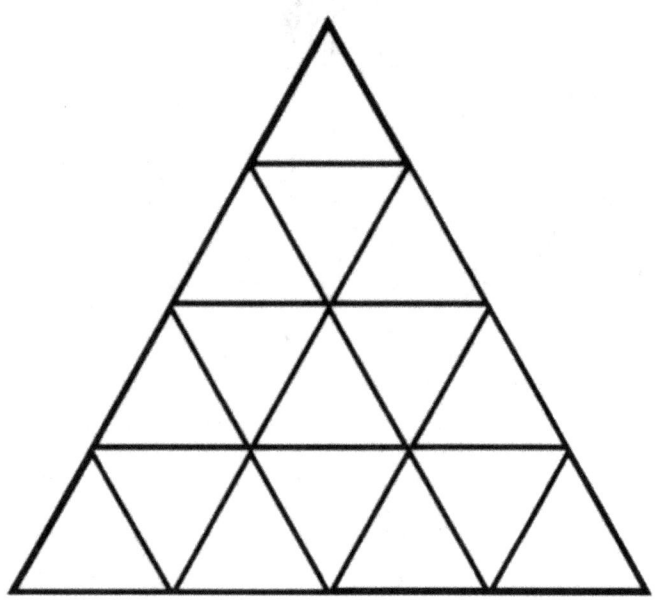

Word Puzzle

Instructions:
Write your explanation to the following story.

A man walks into a bar and asks the bartender for a glass of water. The bartender pulls out a gun and pointed it at the man. The man says "thank you" and walks out.

Alternative Thought Processing

Instructions:
Contemplate the following and think of areas in which common misconceptions or bias influence how security is implemented or approached in your organization.

Given the red dots are areas in which combat aircraft are often hit during engagement, what does the following diagram indicate? What would be your recommendations for additional armoring of the aircraft?

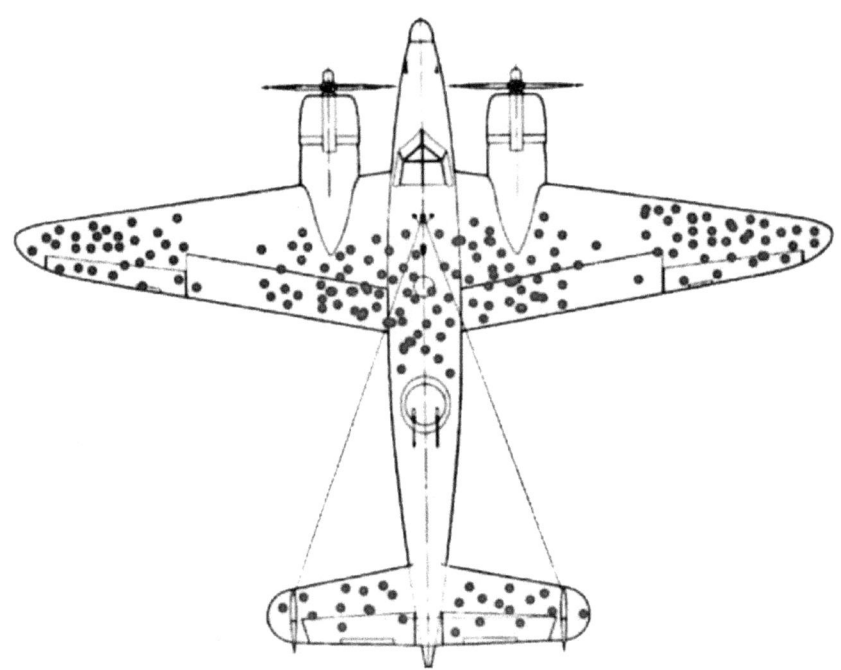

Mindset Challenge Comments and Answers

9 Dot Challenge

Possible answers.

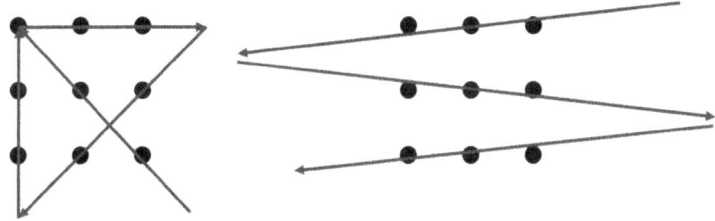

Did you come up with something different? The point of this exercise to support the phrase "think outside the box". Do not limit yourself by what's presented and focus on measuring what "Is" vs what "Should be"

Maze Challenge

Possible Answers

How does your solution compare? The point of this exercise is similar to the prior. Don't let assumptions and limitations prevent possible solutions. A good Red Teamer is able to understand and bend rules in ways that are not always considered.

Triangle Puzzle

Answer: Total Triangles = 27

When faced with a problem for which you don't know the "formula," a brute force approach may be needed. Lessons can be learned, and "formulas" can be added to your knowledge base to improve efficiency when faced with similar problems in the future.

Formula:
```
T(n) = floor(n*(n + 2)*(2n + 1) / 8)
```

Example:
```
f(4) = 4*(4 + 2)*(2*4 + 1) / 8 = 27.000
```

> Reference:
> http://www.billthelizard.com/2009/08/how-many-triangles.html

Word Puzzle

This is a common lateral thinking puzzle. These types of puzzles often gives the audience a seemingly unusual set of circumstances where they must try and figure out what happened or what's going on in an unusual short story. These help show how difficult challenges can often be solved with easy solutions.

Classic Solution:
The man had the hiccups and wanted a glass of water to help get rid of them. The bartender could hear the hiccups when the man spoke, so he brought the gun out to scare the hiccups away. It worked, and the man thanked him and left, no longer needing the glass of water.

How did your answer compare to the classic solution?

Alternative Thought Processing

During World War 2, the U.S. Navy performed a review of aircraft with combat encounters. This review intended to determine where aircraft needed additional armor to ensure survivability and safe return. Upon analysis the Navy decided all the locations where bullet holes were found needed to be better armored as they are more likely to be hit. These included the tips of the wings, the central body, and the elevators.

A Navy Statistician, Abraham Wald[27] had another theory. The areas with bullet holes identified where the aircraft was already survivable. He recommended armoring the nose, engine, and mid-body although few of the aircraft had damage to those areas. Why?

---

[27] "Wald, Abraham. (1943). A Method of Estimating Plane Vulnerability Based on Damage of Survivors. Statistical Research Group, Columbia University. CRC 432" — reprint from July 1980, http://www.dtic.mil/get-tr-doc/pdf?AD=ADA091073&Location=U2&doc=GetTRDoc.pdf.

Wald recognized those areas were also being shot; however, weren't able to return safely. He correctly surmised that aircraft with shots to the wings, central body, and elevators were able to return while those with shots to the nose, engine, and mid-body were catastrophically damaged and unable to return.

Consider how this scenario translates to Red Teaming or security in general. Also consider what is known (and unknown) given information from threat intelligence, current events, and indicators.

Appendix C: Decomposing a Threat Exercise

Description

This exercise walks through the process of decomposing a threat and threat scenario to build a threat profile. You will examine the Energetic Bear threat actor to develop a threat profile that can be used during a Red Team engagement.

Objectives
1. Review the Energetic Bear threat actor's TTPs.
2. Use the information to create a threat that is similar and can be used to support future Red Team engagements.
3. Complete a threat profile template

Exercise Scenario

A client has asked your Red Team to emulate a specific threat. Specifically, they are interested in the attacks by Energetic Bear.

Goal

The goal of this exercise is to create a threat profile document using Energetic Bear for inspiration. As a professional Red Team, you understand that emulating a specific threat actor is not easy or feasible, and focusing on threat TTPs is more relevant. You will use research on Energetic Bear's TTPs to build a custom threat profile that is technically feasible and can be used to engage the client with a realistic threat.

Resources
- MITRE ATT&CK Framework (https://attack.mitre.org/wiki/Main_Page)
- MITRE ATT&CK Navigator (https://attack.mitre.org/wiki/ATT%26CK_Navigator)
- Dragonfly: Cyberespionage Attacks Against Energy Suppliers (http://www.symantec.com/content/en/us/enterprise/media/security_response/whitepapers/Dragonfly_Threat_Against_Western_Energy_Suppliers.pdf)
- Energetic Bear – Crouching Yeti (https://media.kasperskycontenthub.com/wp-content/uploads/sites/58/2018/03/09092926/EB-YetiJuly2014-Public.pdf)
- The Alley of Compromise (https://www.crowdstrike.com/blog/cve-2014-1761-alley-compromise)

Begin the Exercise

Begin by researching the Energetic Bear threat and attack. After you complete your own, compare your observations to the highlights below.

Highlights have been provided to help with this process.

Highlights from the Energetic Bear Threat Actor
- Starting in 2010 and ending in 2014, Energetic Bear / Dragonfly / Crouching Yeti malware attacked numerous computers to collect information on industrial control systems in the United States and Europe
- Spread out over time and thus difficult to detect
- The primary goal was to collect information that impacted the energy and pharmaceutical industries

- Possibly nation-state supported
- Phishing, watering hole attacks
- Known exploits were used (PDF, Java, IE, Word)
- Compromised ICS web servers
- HTTP-based C2
- Specific activities and capabilities

IOCs from the actor Energetic Bear and the HAVEX malware

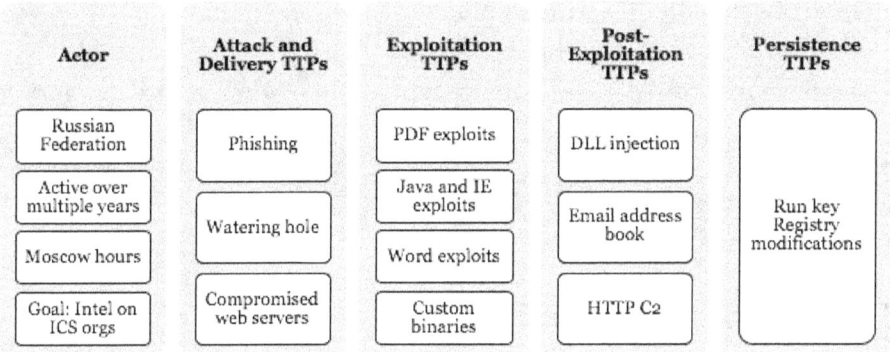

Actor
- Associated with the Russian Federation
- Active over multiple years
- Active primarily during Moscow business hours
- Targeted organizations based in the industry control system sector vGoal of gathering intelligence on ICS-based organizations
- Use of custom malware

Attack and delivery TTPs
- Phishing
- Watering hole
- Compromised web servers

Exploitation TTPs

- PDF exploits
- Java and IE exploits
- Word exploits2
- Custom binaries

Post-exploitation TTPs
- Local system enumeration for OS, username, processes, internet history, etc.
- Scan for known ICS-related ports
- DLL injection to migrate into explorer.exe
- Collect Outlook address book information
- Collect passwords from browsers
- Save exfiltrated data to an encrypted file on disk before delivery to the C2 in an HTTP POST request

Persistence TTPs
Run key registry modifications:

```
HKEY_CURRENT_USER\Software\Microsoft\Windows\CurrentVersion\Run\"TmProvider"

HKEY_LOCAL_MACHINE\SOFTWARE\Microsoft\Windows\CurrentVersion\Run\"TmProvider"

HKEY_LOCAL_MACHINE\ SOFTWARE\Microsoft\Internet Explorer\InternetRegistry\"fertger"

HKEY_LOCAL_MACHINE\SOFTWARE\Microsoft\Internet Explorer\InternetRegistry
```

HAVEX Payload Delivery

Malicious PDF via Spear Phish	Malicious JAR and HTML via Watering Hole	Supply Chain Attack via Legitimate Software
Older PDF exploits	Java 6/7 exploits	Compromise of vendor software
CVE-2011-0611	Internet Explorer 7/8 exploits	

Energetic Bear used three major methods to deliver malware.

1) Malicious PDF via spear-phishing Spear-phishing was used to infect targeted individuals for initial information gathering by delivering malicious PDF documents—in this case, PDF/SWF exploits targeting CVE-2011-0611 to drop malware.3 Even with this running through 2014, older exploits were still valuable.

2) Malicious JAR and HTML via a watering hole attack Watering hole attacks were used to deliver Backdoor.Oldrea by Symantec. These attacks exploited CVE-2013-2465, CVE-2013-1347, and CVE-2012-1723 in Java 6, Java 7, IE 7, and IE 8 to drop the HAVEX malware. The exploits appeared to be modified Metasploit Java exploits built to deliver the HAVEX loader.

3) Legitimate software loaders Energetic Bear compromised several legitimate ICS vendor websites. Binaries such as camera drivers and PLC management software were modified and made to deliver the HAVEX malware.

In order to complete the third attack type, the threat actor had to compromise several ICS vendors' websites. Sometimes called a Strategic Web Compromise (SWC) attack, these have become a favorite attack method from Russian and Chinese-based threats. In this case, SWC attacks were used to compromise a site that would most likely be visited by customers or users of ICS systems. This made the watering hole or binary compromises much more useful against the targeted victim. Using these three attack types demonstrated an organized and arguably sophisticated threat actor. The team behind this planned and organized a scenario to be successful against its target audience.

Once malware was delivered, three major tasks were observed:
- System enumeration tools collected information, such as the OS version, machine name and username, and file and directory listings.
- A credential-harvesting tool extracted stored passwords from various web browsers.
- Secondary implants6 communicated with different C2 infrastructures using custom protocols and payloads executed in memory.

HAVEX HTTP Request Sample
POST Request

```
POST /wp08/wp-
includes/dtcla.php?id=285745296322896178920098FD80-
20&v1=038&v2=170393861&q=5265882854508EFCF958F979E4
HTTP/1.1
User-Agent: Mozilla/5.0 (Windows; U; Windows NT 6.1; en-
US) AppleWebKit/525.19(KHTML, like Gecko)
Chrome/1.0.154.36 Safari/525.19
Host: toons.freesexycomics.com
Content-Length: 0
Cache-Control: no-cache
```

Post Response

```
HTTP/1.1 200 OK
Date: Wed, 22 Jan 2014 13:40:48 GMT
Content-Type: text/html
Transfer-Encoding: chunked
Connection: keep-alive
Server: Apache/1.3.37 (Unix)
Cache-Control: no-cache

9f65
<html><head><mega http-equiv='CACHE-CONTROL'
content='NO-CACHE'></head><body>No data!<!--
havexQlpoOTFBWSZTWWYvDI0BOsD////////////////////////
////////////////4oB+93VVXu69DuN7XYzds9yt49Ques
[...TRUNCATED ...]
```

```
+yUW3zfTxWAOstsCwCckdW5
AH5Q6vbbCu7GputPt5CSfgPCAKXcAOOICMsqliACGYEhAQT3v9eD
M92D/8XckU4UJBmLwyNA==havex--></body></head>
```

In this example from Symantec, several indicators can be identified.

The POST request shows several indicators that may be incorporated into an emulated threat:
- A target PHP file (dtcla.php)
- Interesting URL parameters (id, v1, v2, q)
- A potentially interesting User-Agent
- A target host

Like the request, the response has several indicators:
- A server header
- A potentially unique ID (9f65)
- Base64-encoded data stored between text (havex < base64 > havex)

Note: MALWAREMUSTDIE2 posted a great write-up on the HAVEX malware. This provides additional examples of C2 source code and HTTP request/response pairs. Reference: http://pastebin.com/qCdMwtZ6

Create a threat profile

1) Use the research you conducted and this information to create a threat profile. There is no right or wrong answer. The important components of a threat profile are technical feasibility, ability to meet engagement goals, and ability to implement using your Red Team's tools and ability.

Tips
- Profiles must be technically feasible. If your profile calls for the use of zero-days, make sure you can deliver. (white carding and assumed breach models may help)
- Threat profiles are implemented as part of the C2 plan. They directly influence the selection and configuration of C2. Always

consider the technical capabilities and limitations of your C2 platforms when designing a profile

2) Develop your profile using the following template then compare to the possible solution.

Category	Description
Description	
Goal and Intent	
Key IOCs	
C2 Overview	
TTPs (Enumeration, Delivery, Lateral Movement, Privilege Escalation, etc.)	
Exploitation	
Persistence	

Possible Solution

Category	Description
Description	General mid-tiered threat that uses common offensive tools and techniques.
Goal and Intent	Exist in the network to enumerate systems and information in order to maintain Command and Control to support future attacks.
Key IOCs	PowerShell Empire HTTP agent on TCP 80, Location: Memory Resident and PowerShell Script stored in Registry, HTTP matching HAVEX
C2 Overview	HTTPS on port 80 with a 5 second callback. Calling directly to threat-owned domains.
TTPs (Enumeration, Delivery, Lateral Movement, Privilege Escalation, etc.)	Initially delivered during exploitation. POST exploitation delivery via PowerShell commands. Enumeration and lateral movement via PS Empire and native Windows commands. Privilege escalation limited and determined POST exploitation.
Exploitation	Social Engineering via Phishing, watering hole, and supply chain via compromised web servers
Persistence	Persistence via registry RUN key modification

Think about the following questions:

How does your solution compare?

Do you have the technical ability to execute this profile?

Did you copy the exact techniques from the reference example, or did you fill in the gaps with other techniques?

Are you prepared to explore unfamiliar techniques to better mimic the reference example?

Glossary of Terms

Assumed Breach
The Assumed Breach Model assumes a threat has some level of access to a target at the initiation of the engagement.

This model is arguably the most beneficial of all the models. The threat is assumed to have some level of access to a target before beginning. This starts a scenario much further into the attack timeline. Assuming someone can breach a network is often argued by less mature organizations. Those who say "prove it" will often not like this scenario. Less mature organizations assume that threats must prove they can get in before beginning. When is the proof important? It is important only if measuring the ability a threat has to "get in" is important. If this is not a key goal, using the Assumed Breach Model will save time and money. It will free the Red Team to explore higher impact goals.

Blue Cell
The blue cell is the opposite side of red. Is it all the components defending a target network. The blue cell is typically comprised of blue team members, defenders, internal staff, and an organization's management.

Blue Team
A security team that defends against threats.

Command and Control (C2)
Command and Control (C2) is the influence an attacker has over a compromised computer system that they control.

C2 Tiers
Designing a robust C2 infrastructure involves creating multiple layers of Command and Control. These can be described as tiers. Each tier offers a

level of capability and covertness. The idea of using multiple tiers is the same as not putting all your eggs in one basket. If C2 is detected and blocked, having a backup will allow operations to continue.

C2 tiers generally fall into three categories: Interactive, Short Haul, and Long Haul. These are sometimes labeled as Tier 1, 2, or 3. There is nothing unique to each tier other than how they are to be used.

Interactive tier
- Used for general commands, enumeration, scanning, data exfiltration, etc.
- This tier has the most interaction and is at the greatest risk of exposure.
- Plan to lose access from communication failure, agent failure, or Blue Team actions.
- Run enough interactive sessions to maintain access. Although interactive, this doesn't mean blasting the client with packets. Use good judgment to minimize interaction just enough to perform an action.

Short haul tier

- Used as a backup to reestablish interactive sessions.
- Use covert communications that blend in with the target.
- Slow callback times. Callback times in the 1–24 hr. range are common.

Long haul tier

- The same as Short Haul but even lower and slower.
- Slow callback times. Callback times of 24+ hours are common.

Deconfliction

Deconfliction is the ability to identify which activity is generated by a Red Team and which is not. In general, the deconfliction provide a way to separate Red Team activity from real-world activity through a controlled process.

Engagement / Exercise Control Group (ECG)
The Engagement (or Exercise) Control Group is ultimately responsible for all activities conducted during the engagement. Most often, the Engagement Control Group is composed of one or two senior managers from the target environment (for example a Chief Information Officer or Chief Operating Officer), one member from the Information Technology department of the environment, a White Cell liaison, and a Red Team liaison. More may be added as required. All must be Trusted Agents.

Exfiltration
Exfiltration is the extraction of information from a target. This is typically through a covert channel.

Get In, Stay In, Act
The three main phases of a Red Team engagement.

> Get In
>
> Gain access to a network. The Red Team must have access to their target. Access can be through a legitimate compromise or access is directly granted as part of an assumed breach scenario, such as an insider threat scenario
>
> Stay In
>
> Establish persistence or a permanent presence. Red Team engagements are typically longer than other types of tests. A Red Team usually establishes persistence or a permanent presence in order to survive the duration of the engagement.

Act
Phase where a Red Team performs operational impacts against a target.

IOC (Indicator of Compromise)
Indicators of Compromise (IOCs) are artifacts that identify or describe threat actions.

OPFOR
An Opposing Force, or enemy force, that is typically used by the military in war-gaming scenarios. Red Teams are commonly associated with or support an OPFOR in war-gaming scenarios.

OPLOG (Operator Log)
Operator logs are the records generated by Red Team operators during an engagement. These logs have specific and required fields that must be captured.

Operational Impact
An operational impact is the effect of a goal-driven action within a target environment.

OPSEC
OPSEC or Operational Security is a process that identifies critical information to determine if friendly actions can be observed by enemy intelligence, determines if information obtained by adversaries could be interpreted to be useful to them, and then executes selected measures that eliminate or reduce adversary exploitation of friendly critical information. In terms of Red Teaming, it is understanding what actions Blue can observe and minimizes exposure.

Outbrief, Executive

The first post-engagement meeting is usually the executive outbrief. An executive brief is typically performed soon after execution completes (within one or two days following execution). This meeting is tailored toward management and should include key personnel from the target organization. The outcome of a Red Team engagement may impact how an organization operates in the future, potentially requiring funding to pursue mitigations or staffing modifications. Management awareness and buy-in are critical if Red Team results will be used to improve an organization's security stance to defend and respond to a threat.

Outbrief, Technical
The technical outbrief (aka a tech-on-tech) is a bi-directional technical exchange of information between the Red Team, the Blue Team, and the organization. During this exchange, both the Red and the defensive elements provide a highly detailed, step-by-step technical review of the actions and results (including all associated details) of the engagement. This is where training and education meet and is one of the most valuable opportunities for all parties to learn.

Persistence
Persistence is the ability or techniques used to establish a permanent presence in order to survive the duration of the engagement.

Prepositioning
Prepositioning is the process of using the access and capabilities gained during an engagement to best position an operator for the execution of an impact.

Red Cell
The term red cell is borrowed from the military. It is commonly associated with a group that plays OPFOR (opposing force) during red vs. blue exercises. A red cell is the components that make up the offensive portion of a red team engagement that simulates the strategic and tactical

responses of a given target. The red cell is typically comprised of red team leads and operators and is commonly referred to as Red Team instead of Red Cell.

Red Team
A Red Team is an independent group that, from the perspective of a threat or adversary, explores alternative plans and operations to challenge an organizatioøn to improve its effectiveness.

Red Team Lead
Serves as the operational and administrative lead for the Red Team. Conducts engagement, budget, and resource management for the Red Team, Provides oversight and guidance for engagements, capabilities, and technologies. Ensures adherence to all laws, regulations, policies, and Rules of Engagement.

Red Team Operator
Complies with all Red Team requirements under the direction of the Red Team Lead. Operational executor of the engagement. Applies Red Team TTPs to the engagement. Provides technical research and capability to the Red Team. Keeps detailed logs during each phase of the engagement. Provides log and information support for creation of the final report

Rules of Engagement (ROE)
The Rules of Engagement establish the responsibilities, relationships, and guidelines among the Red Team, the customer, the system owner, and any stakeholders required for engagement execution.

Situational Awareness
Situational awareness is a step in a Red Team engagement used gather as much information as needed on the targets and target environment. The information gathered is used to determine the next actions towards privilege escalation, lateral movement, or other steps. It is is a key

component to Red Teaming and should be performed to some level on all access targets.

Threat
A threat is an expression of intention to inflict evil, injury, or damage.

Threat Emulation
Threat Emulation Threat Emulation is the process of mimicking the TTPs of a specific threat.

Threat Intelligence
Threat intelligence is information that has been aggregated, transformed, analyzed, interpreted, or enriched to provide the context for decision-making processes regarding threats.

Threat Model
A threat model is the process by which potential threats or the absence of appropriate safeguards, can be identified, enumerated, and mitigations can be prioritized.

Threat Perspective
a Threat's Perspective is the threat's initial point of view. This perspective is used to build and shape a threat profile or scenario. A threat's perspective may be that of an outsider, nearsider, or insider.

Threat Profile
A threat profile is used to establish the rules as to how a Red Team will act and operate. These rules serve as a roadmap for a Red Team by guiding how and what type of actions should be performed. Threat profiles are a key part of developing and designing C2 early in Red Team planning.

Threat Scenario

Scenarios provide insight into how a defensive solution will perform and conform to the processes, procedures, policies, activities, personnel, organizations, environment, threats, constraints, assumptions, and support involved in the security mission. Scenarios generally describe the role of the threat, how it will interact with the systems and networks within the target environment, and elicits real-world truth of how essential internal practices are employed. In short, it answers how the target's security operations would dynamically perform an action to deliver results, outputs, or prove capability.

Tradecraft
Tradecraft is the techniques and procedures of espionage. Tradecraft is typically associated with the intelligence community. TTPs and Tradecraft are used interchangeably in this course.

Trusted Agent (TA)
The Trusted Agent's primary role is to limit irreversible damage and risk to life, limb, eyesight, and equipment; however, they are more often used to prevent the defenders from causing unexpected self-inflicted damage.

A Trusted Agent (TA) has privileged and detailed knowledge of engagement activities, milestones, conditions, and the engagement status that would unduly bias or influence the actions of the environment staff and defenders. A Trusted Agent must protect all information from being provided to any party without the express approval of the Engagement Control Group.

TTPs
TTPs are Tactics, Techniques and Procedures (sometimes called Tools, Techniques, and Procedures).

Two Person Integrity (TPI)
Two-person integrity is used to verify activities performed during the engagement and should be maintained at all times. A team member should

review, understand, and provide a "sanity check" for each action/command performed. TPI reduce personal and engagement risks.

Web Shell
A web shell is a piece of web code that is placed on an Web server to allow an adversary to use the Web server as a gateway into a network. Web shells are commonly deployed as part of an application security attack.

White Cell
Serves as referee between Red Team activities and defender responses during an engagement. Controls the engagement environment/network. Monitors adherence to the ROE. Coordinates activities required to achieve engagement goals. Correlates Red Team activities with defensive actions. Ensures the engagement is conducted without bias to either side.

www.ingramcontent.com/pod-product-compliance
Lightning Source LLC
Chambersburg PA
CBHW052349220526
45465CB00003BA/1025